AN

HISTORICAL DISCOURSE

IN COMMEMORATION OF THE

ONE HUNDREDTH ANNIVERSARY

OF THE FORMATION OF THE

FIRST CONGREGATIONAL CHURCH IN TEMPLETON,

MASSACHUSETTS.

With an Appendix,

EMBRACING A SURVEY OF THE MUNICIPAL AFFAIRS OF THE TOWN.

BY

EDWIN G. ADAMS,

JUNIOR PASTOR.

BOSTON:

CROSBY, NICHOLS, AND COMPANY,

111, WASHINGTON STREET.

1857.

BOSTON:
PRINTED BY JOHN WILSON AND SON,
22, SCHOOL STREET.

PREFACE.

As it seemed desirable to make some commemoration of so interesting an event as the completion of the first century of the existence of the First Church of Christ in this town, the junior pastor, on Sunday, Dec. 9, 1855, the day preceding the anniversary, preached a Discourse, continued through both parts of the day, containing an historical sketch of the early settlement of the town and of the annals of the church. Rev. Dr. WELLINGTON, the senior pastor, took part in the services, morning and afternoon,—reading the Scriptures and hymns, and offering prayers.

Soon after the delivery of the Discourse, a request was made to have it printed; and arrangements were made for that purpose. But, before they were carried into execution, the desire was expressed, from many sources, that the writer should proceed to make some account also of the municipal affairs of the town since its incorporation. He assented to this in part, though not expecting, at first, to enter into so much detail as is done in the Appendix. The printing of the sermon has accordingly been delayed, in order that the whole might appear together. The amount of time and investigation requisite to make and verify a sketch of the affairs of a town and society, extending through a period of a hundred years, can be appreciated only by those who have performed similar labors. Often a brief statement, occupying perhaps but a line, especially when it involves the assertion of a negative, is the result of hours and days of research among records sometimes not very legible. It has been the author's aim to make the survey contained in the following pages include a correct account of all the important votes and doings recorded on the various subjects named. For this purpose, he has carefully examined all the warrants ever issued for meetings of the inhabitants of this town, and for meetings of the ancient proprietors and of the parish, with the votes passed, and action taken under each of them. In the Discourse, some passages omitted in the delivery, for want of time, are now inserted; and several additions have been made, consisting chiefly of historical details. A few items, originally in the Discourse, have been placed in the Appendix.

The information respecting the value of land in the township in the early times was obtained mainly through the courtesy of DANIEL WARD, Esq., the examiner of titles in the Registry of Deeds at Worcester. Assistance in ascertaining various other facts has also been afforded by Rev. JOHN L. SIBLEY, Librarian of Harvard College; by Rev. Dr. WELLINGTON; and by others.

CONTENTS.

APPENDIX, *continued.*

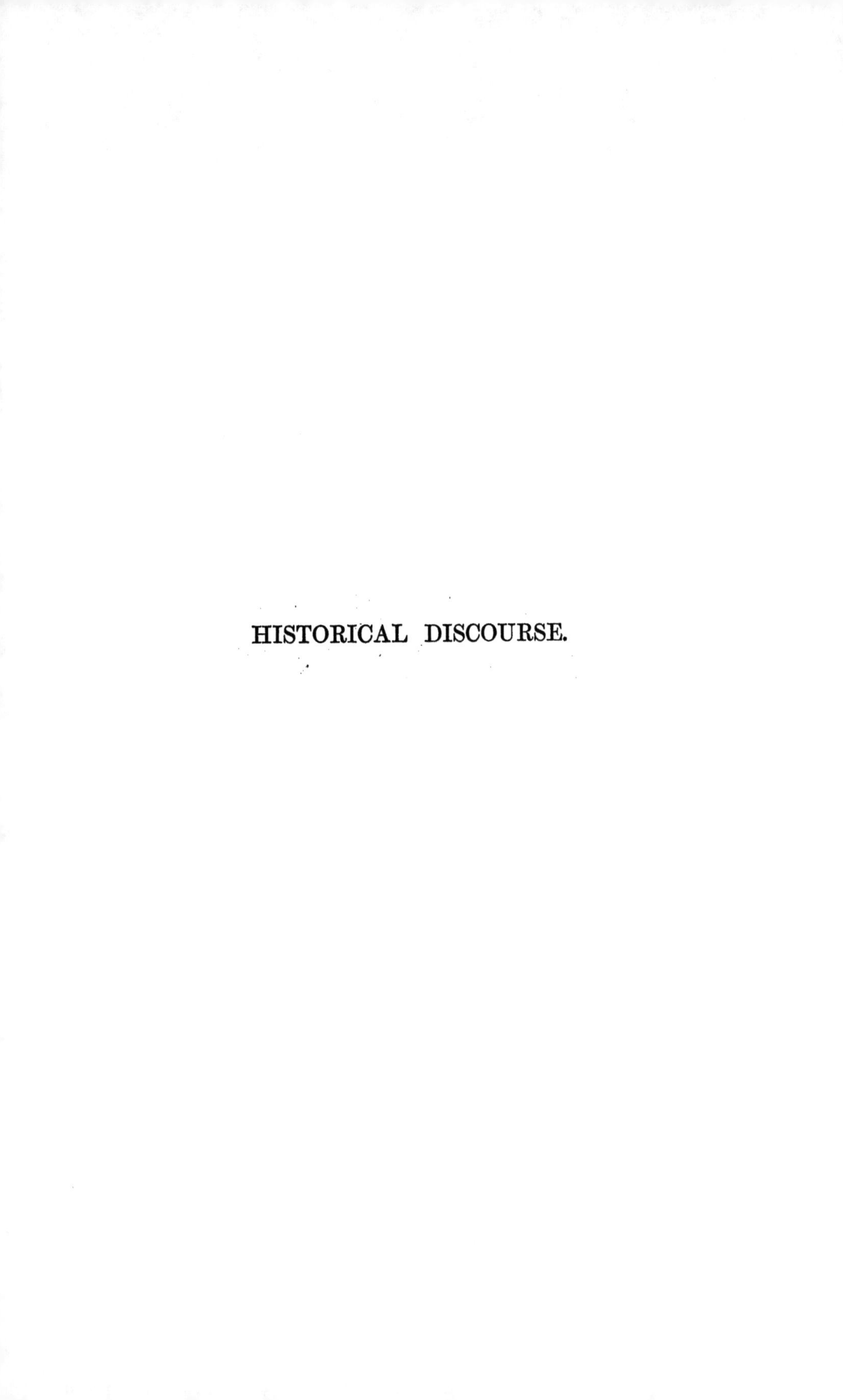

HISTORICAL DISCOURSE.

HISTORICAL DISCOURSE.

Ps. xliv. 1, and lxxviii. 4: "WE HAVE HEARD WITH OUR EARS, O GOD! OUR FATHERS HAVE TOLD US, WHAT WORK THOU DIDST IN THEIR DAYS, IN THE TIMES OF OLD." — "WE WILL NOT HIDE THEM FROM THEIR CHILDREN; SHOWING TO THE GENERATION TO COME THE PRAISES OF THE LORD, AND HIS STRENGTH, AND HIS WONDERFUL WORKS THAT HE HATH DONE."

THIS congregation has come together to-day with memories and sacred associations filling our minds that are fitted to take a deep hold on the feelings. We have arrived, as you know, at the close of the first century of the existence of our religious organizations. It is a hundred years since the first permanent establishment was made of gospel-institutions within the territory of this town, by the formation of this church of Christ, and the first settlement of a minister here. Standing now at the point of such a deeply interesting anniversary, our feelings cannot but be in harmony with the sentiment of the texts just read. How could we properly employ our thoughts in the house of God, on this day, except by looking *backward* to the times of the fathers, — to their noble struggles, their high and worthy views and purposes, and the things wrought in their days; by looking also *upward* to the all-controlling and good providence of God, by which events have been guided, and his people blessed; and looking *forward* to the future opening upon us, with its new privileges, duties, and hopes?

If we go back a hundred and twenty-five years, we find the interior parts of Massachusetts then almost wholly unoccupied by human beings. Throughout the more hilly portion of the State, between the Wachusett Ridge and the meadows of the Connecticut River, every thing remained in a state of nature. It was all one vast and dense forest, majestic in its noble growth of the pine, the chestnut, the oak, and many other native trees. Within the profound shades dwelt unmolested the wild beasts; and the wilderness blossomed in beauty, unhelped by the hand of man. Even the native tribes of Indians had very few permanent homes within the region: they ranged over this part of the country for hunting and fishing, but built their wigwams in the more favorable places by the seaside and in the rich valleys.

In this township, it is not known that there were any cultivated grounds or permanent habitations of the red man. There was really no Indian title to extinguish, because none of that race had actually occupied the soil. There were none even to *claim* property in it. Very few traces of so much as their wandering presence here have ever been found. An arrow-head or two have been picked up. A stone-mortar and pestle for pounding corn was once found on the banks of Trout Brook. The oldest traditions of the town indicate no signs of any aboriginal dwelling-places, with a single exception, — that of a long-deserted Indian abode, the remains of which were discovered, in early times, in a sheltered spot within the present bounds of Phillipston. It is believed that no traces of their graves have ever been seen here.

A little more than a century ago, the frontier towns of the white man in this part of the State were Brookfield, Lancaster, and Lunenburg; and then the wilderness was unsettled till the fertile grounds along the Connecticut River were reached, where were the towns of Northfield, Deerfield, and Hadley. But enterprising men from the more eastern section had passed over the country, and marked its advantages. There were many disposed to avail themselves of new lands for settlement. There were sturdy hearts among the young men, glad to think of planting for themselves a home where they might bring the ones they loved, and where they could cultivate broad acres to call *their own.* The General Court of the Province of Massachusetts was glad to give away these lands in the hill-country for the sake of having new townships opened. Those who had done service in King Philip's War, as it was called, against the Narraganset tribe of Indians, having made claim for compensation, the General Court, first in 1728, and afterwards in 1732, granted several townships, each of six miles square, for those soldiers and their heirs, to be divided into lots for a hundred and twenty proprietors in each township, who were to apportion to each other their respective shares. The law also enacted, that sixty families should be settled in each place, with a minister of the gospel, within seven years from the date of the grant; reserving in each township one right of lands for the first minister, one for the support of the ministry in coming times, and one for the support of schools.* Two of these seven townships were finally laid out here, — one called Narraganset No. 2, which is now the town of Westminster; the other called Narraganset No. 6, which included Templeton and the greater part of the present town of Phillipston. Township No. 1 was in Maine. At least one other of the townships granted at this time is said to have been also in Maine; and two seem to have been laid out within the present bounds of New Hampshire, on territory then claimed erroneously by Massachusetts. It is said that the whole body of claimants under the grant for Narraganset soldiers met at Boston, on the Common, June, 1732, and lots were drawn for the respective townships. Our proprietors did not like their first location, and obtained leave to change it for the territory here. Not far from the same time, grants were made by the General Court, on similar conditions, — chiefly to other claimants for services against the Indians, — of the lands in the present

* See Appendix A.

townships of Athol, Petersham, Barre, Winchendon, Ashburnham, and Royalston. Some of the grantees came here in person: many sold their rights for small sums. But there was not much progress in settling any of these towns for fifteen or twenty years at least after those grants by the Legislature; and, in some cases, the time was extended by the General Court, within which the proprietors might fulfil the conditions prescribed. The war between France and England had involved the Colonies. The French, then holding possession of Canada, encouraged the Indians in the northern parts of New England to make inroads upon the scattered frontier settlements of the English, — burning and killing. In such times, it required brave men and strong-hearted women to come and plant themselves in the wilderness. And all the more because our fathers were led through such a severe discipline as that by which they were here tried, in many particulars, did they learn to feel the presence of the Divine Power and Goodness; learn to fear God, and not to fear *man.*

According to the facts now stated, it came to pass, that, throughout this whole section of country, it is just about a hundred years since permanent civil and Christian institutions were planted: in some towns it is now a little more; in others, a little less. Till a sufficient number of inhabitants could be brought in to form a town-organization for civil purposes, it was a necessity that the affairs of the settlement should be managed by the proprietors who held the grant of the soil in the respective townships. The number of rights in this town was a hundred and twenty: in a few cases, one person held two or more rights. The owners of these rights were made a body corporate for the purpose of managing the settlement. They had legal powers similar to inhabitants of towns. They could lay taxes for establishing roads and schools, for supporting public worship, and for other purposes. These taxes were assessed wholly on the land, and not on personal property nor polls. Previous to incorporation as a town, all proprietors of the township, wherever they might reside, could vote in its affairs. Our proprietors, it appears, lived mostly in the towns of Concord, Groton, Lancaster (especially that part of Lancaster then called Chockset, now Sterling), Bolton, Littleton, Westford, Chelmsford, Stowe, Marlborough, Billerica, and Woburn. Their earliest recorded meeting as an incorporation was held at Concord, Oct. 29, 1733. At this meeting they chose Samuel Chandler, Esq., of Concord, Jonas Houghton, of Lancaster probably, and John Longley, of Groton, a committee "to lay out a township on the back of Rutland, in lieu of one assigned to us west of Ponocook and Suncook."

At a meeting at Concord, Dec. 3, 1733, they accepted the township thus laid out, and chose a committee "to finish the line and burn the woods till further order." But though the proprietors chose their officers, and sent men here — "into the woods," as the records significantly call it — to survey and explore so early as 1733 and 1734, yet it was not till almost twenty years later that any substantial progress was made in bringing forward the actual settlement. Not only the difficulties of the wilderness were in the way, but also the French and Indian hostilities which raged between 1744 and 1749.

In 1746, one of the Athol settlers was killed by Indians. The same year, a fort, built for the protection of settlers in the town of Adams, Berkshire County, was besieged and taken by a large body of French and Indians. In 1747, the inhabitants of Ashburnham (then called Dorchester-Canada) abandoned their town for fear of the enemy. In the spring of that year, a man in Athol was taken prisoner by the savages, and carried to Canada. Garrisons of soldiers were for some years stationed by the government in the frontier towns to protect the people. In July, 1748, the house of Mr. John Fitch, in Ashby (who was the first settler of that place, and from whom the town of Fitchburg, it is said, derives its name), was attacked by a party of eighty Indians. The house was occupied by Mr. Fitch, his wife, five children, and three soldiers stationed there for defence. On the morning of that day, two of the soldiers had gone a few miles away; one of them, returning, was fired upon and killed. Mr. Fitch and the remaining soldier defended the house for some hours; Mrs. Fitch loading the guns as fast as they fired. At length the soldier was killed by an Indian's shot. Mr. Fitch then agreed to surrender, the foe promising to spare their lives. The Indians then burned the house, taking a little plunder; and carried Mr. and Mrs. Fitch and the five children — marching on foot — as captives to Canada, in order to obtain money from the French. The whole family finally returned to Massachusetts. It is related that a log-chain, taken at Mr. Fitch's house, was carried by one of the Indians on his shoulders all the way to Canada: there he sold it for rum. Such hostilities were suspended, for a few years, after the treaty of Aix-la-Chapelle, which was negotiated in 1748.

Surveys had been made here, however, at an early day; and one division of land among the proprietors completed, by laying out to each a lot of about forty acres "of the best of the upland." These were called "house-lots," and the division was made in 1735.* These sections were intended to be of nearly equal quality; and they were numbered, and distributed to the proprietors by drawing lots. Some of the owners came here and labored, especially in the summer season, previous to 1750. Something was done towards roads, by marking trees, or clearing them away. Steps had been taken, though at first with but indifferent success, to provide a sawmill. But before 1750, probably, there were almost or quite no houses or families established here, owing to the causes just mentioned. From that time, families began to move in. It had been voted, that the sixty families who

---

* See Appendix B.

would first settle on their lots should receive a certain sum, amounting, however, to only a few dollars each; the other sixty "non-settlers" paying the money into the proprietors' treasury for them. The earliest payment from the treasury to any person, for thus building a house on his lot and living in it with a family, was made in September, 1751, to Elias Wilder; the next in October, 1751, to Deacon Charles Baker; and the next in May, 1752, to Timothy Chase. In the course of three years and a half afterwards, such payments had been made, in all, to about thirty actual settlers. This includes, it will be observed, settlements anywhere within the whole township, — the part now in Phillipston, as well as in Templeton. And from that day to this, through the whole of the hundred years, the number of inhabitants in this territory has been constantly increasing.

Those original proprietors and settlers were persons whose views were liberal, enlightened, and honest. They came here to labor with their hands, in the pursuit of an honorable livelihood, relying on the bounties of that Providence which they knew would preserve seedtime and harvest. They were seeking no sudden influx of wealth from trade and speculations, or by digging for hidden treasures or ores. They expected to work hard, — they and their families. All they did looked forward to permanency; for they felt, that, when their generation had passed away, they should leave a goodly heritage to the coming times. They meant to lay the foundation of prosperity for the town on the basis of industry, economy, and frugality; on intelligence, sobriety, and Christian principle.

They relied, we have said, on the cultivation of the soil, and its growth of timber. There had been rumors, indeed, of something remarkable and precious in the locality. There was a spot called Mine Hill, and there were other places, where rocks had been found of yellow and shining appearance. Some thought there might be large profits yet out of digging for such treasure. In those early times, one of the first inquiries, whenever a new region was explored anywhere in New England, was, "Are there any precious ores there?" But our oldest records contain an evident proof of the good sense of our proprietors on that subject. At a meeting on the 8th of June, 1743, held at Concord, there was an article in the warrant in these words, — "to act as the said proprietors shall think proper concerning *the mines* in said township." But they voted, in these positive words, "that the article be entirely dismissed for the present." It was never renewed.* Their attention was turned to more practicable matters. A road was marked from the township to Narraganset No. 2, that is, Westminster. Committees were authorized to buy lands that had before been lotted out to individuals, in order that the settlers might secure mill-privileges. Only a few years after the first organization, they engaged Mr. Sheldon to build a sawmill. They early chose out a place for the meeting-house. In 1744, they

---

* See Appendix C.

voted to lay a road from the meeting-house place to the sawmill, and thence onward toward Westminster. However, Mr. Sheldon could not build the sawmill, as was expected; and a bargain was made to give land to others who agreed to build a mill. The first sawmill seems to have been erected just before the French and Indian War of 1744, already spoken of, and to have lain neglected for some years during those hostilities; no permanent inhabitants coming in till the peace. It was then found not to be in good working order; for, in 1749, the clerk was directed to write to the owners "to rectify the sawmill." But, as it never proved satisfactory, another was built not many years after. We have said that houses seem to have been first erected and occupied by families in 1750 or 1751; and within two years more, as soon as there were twenty families or thereabouts in the township, it was determined to build a meeting-house, fifty feet long by forty wide.

The Lord's Day was respected from the very beginning. Before the meeting-house was built, and at a time when the congregations in the neighboring settlements at Athol, Petersham, and elsewhere, felt obliged to carry their weapons with them, when assembled for public worship, for fear of Indians, and the ministers preached with a loaded gun by their side, did the settlers here regularly assemble in private houses to consecrate the day with psalm and prayer, and listen to the preacher's discourse. In the autumn of 1752, when there were probably not more than fifteen or eighteen families in the township, the proprietors granted a tax of four shillings on each right of land to provide preaching for the ensuing winter. This was a far larger sum, in proportion to the property then here, than what is now paid for the support of public worship in this town by all denominations. In 1753, they did the same. Rev. Aaron Whitney, of Petersham, and Mr. Boaz Brown, were the committee to obtain a preacher. They employed Dr. Joseph Lord, of Athol, then called Pequoiage, who was a physician and preacher, a man of good ability, and the most prominent person among the settlers of that township. He was the first and only preacher employed here till Rev. Mr. Pond came. Dr. Lord was son of Rev. Joseph Lord, who was minister at Charleston, S.C. He was graduated at Harvard University in 1726; and practised medicine in the town of Sunderland, previous to his residence in Athol. He afterwards removed to Vermont, and was a judge of a county court. He died in Westmoreland, N.H., in 1788.*

As soon as the meeting-house was finished, it was determined to settle a minister, and make ready for all the institutions on which they relied for the prosperity of the town. About the same time, a grist-mill was built by Mr. Thomas Sawyer, by help of a tax on each lot granted by the proprietors. From the survey of the records and history of the town up to the point when these things were first executed

---

* These facts concerning Mr. Lord's life are taken from Rev. Samuel F. Clarke's Centennial Discourse at Athol.

a hundred years ago, we cannot but be struck with a sense of the enlarged and far-sighted views of those earliest settlers. What objects were their greatest sacrifices immediately aimed at? What were they most anxious to secure? To what did they devote every dollar they could spare, or gain by extra labors? Clearly, the four great things they were most resolved upon in their public affairs, and determined to have, whatever else they might go without, were roads, mills, schools, and church institutions. And now that a hundred years have rolled on, and our Commonwealth has increased so much in population; has so vastly enlarged its wealth, multiplied its comforts of living, and gained such an honorable fame over the whole world for the intelligence and character of its citizens, for its principles of civil liberty and of religion, — tell me from what sources of public effort have sprung this wondrous prosperity, this intelligence and honorable character, and the abounding charities of the sons and daughters of Massachusetts? While relying as our fathers did, under Providence, upon the annual fertility of the soil, as the great source from which sustenance comes, has not this great expansion of the prosperity of the husbandman and of all classes been precisely owing to the surpassing interest manifested by our State in just those same four subjects? that is to say, first, in improving the means of communication by common roads, and at length by steam transportation; secondly, by looking to the advantages of machinery in situations to be driven by the vast water-power of our State; thirdly, by cherishing public free schools; and, fourthly, by steadily upholding the institutions of public worship, and of Christianity in all its applications.

Depend upon it, that while the earliest settlers of this township made such exertions and sacrifices (amid all the difficulties of first bringing the forest under cultivation) for the sake of means of travel and transport, for mills, schools, and the church, they were directly and powerfully co-operating with just those instrumentalities and principles which have made in our Commonwealth, out of a little one, such a great people. Thus the fathers were working for the future, rather than for their own times. With enlightened views, heroic purposes, and steadfast faith, they were acting in harmony with the eternal laws and plans of the Almighty's moral providence; and therefore mighty success followed their labors.

In proceeding now to trace the succession of things here in the century past, with especial reference to our church history and religious institutions, let us first fix clearly in the mind a few of the important dates and events. Though the township was granted some twenty years earlier, it is now just a hundred years ago that families enough had settled here, under the regulations of the proprietors, to begin religious institutions, having just builded a meeting-house; Phillipston and Templeton being then together.

The first meeting-house stood upwards of fifty

years, and until this house in which we are now assembled was built, which was in 1811. On the 10th of December, 1755, the First Church of Christ was embodied, and a minister was ordained, — the Rev. DANIEL POND. His ministry, however, lasted only three or four years, and produced, consequently, but little impression upon the town. Very soon after, another minister was settled, — the Rev. EBENEZER SPARHAWK, who came here in the year 1761, while there were not more, probably, than about fifty or sixty families in the whole township (the west or Phillipston part included, as well as the Templeton): that was also before the place was incorporated with town-privileges. Mr. Sparhawk continued in the ministry here as long as he lived; that is, to Nov. 25, 1805, when it wanted only fifteen days of completing the first half-century of the church. Fifteen months after Mr. Sparhawk's death, the Rev. CHARLES WELLINGTON was ordained, and continues — God be thanked! — pastor and minister to this day. So that our whole ecclesiastical history, from the beginning, naturally divides itself into two great periods, each of just half a century. The first comprises the fifty years succeeding the formation of the church, — almost the whole of which was covered by Rev. Mr. Sparhawk's ministry; the second period comprises the fifty years since Mr. Sparhawk's death, — almost the whole of which also is covered by the ministry of his immediate successor, Rev. Dr. Wellington. Let it be further observed, that Templeton, having been incorporated as a town a year or two after Mr. Sparhawk's ordination here, the territory at first belonging to Templeton, which is now in Phillipston, was set off as a distinct precinct or parish in 1774; and that territory, with some addition from Athol, was at length incorporated as a town in the year 1786, originally bearing the name of Gerry, but since changed to Phillipston. A church was gathered there in 1785; twenty-five of the members of which at first belonged to this church, and were dismissed for the purpose of forming that new church. Not far from the same period, also, — that is, when about half of the time of Mr. Sparhawk's ministry had passed, — there was a Baptist church-organization established in Templeton, to which about twenty of the members of the First Church withdrew. The parallel between the two half-century periods continued; for, when about half of the time of the present senior pastor's ministry had expired, namely, in the year 1832, and just fifty years after the formation of that Baptist church, there was also another division, by the organization in this town of "the Trinitarian Church," to which about twenty-five members withdrew from the First Church.

With these prominent facts and dates distinctly in mind, you will now be prepared to take a cursory and comprehensive glance through the whole period of our ecclesiastical history.

Looking back, then, a hundred years, we find those resolute men who were the pioneers here completing their preparations to worship God in freedom, according to their own consciences. We see them relying on the great Protestant principle, that the Scriptures are to every man, who sincerely strives to walk by their light, a sufficient rule of faith and practice. They wanted no bishop nor presbytery to rule over them. They were competent, as freemen in Christ, to gather themselves into a church, and to appoint and ordain one to be their minister in the things of the gospel. In the year 1755, so early as the 8th of January, they signed their names, together with their pastor elect, — to the number of twelve men in all, — to a church covenant; professing their determination, as disciples of the Lord Jesus, to walk together, as a church of Christ, in mutual charity, and obedience to gospel rules and the use of Christian privileges. Though this was done in the early part of the year, the organization of the church was not considered as completed till the concurrence and fellowship of the Christian brethren of the neighborhood had been manifested. The council convened for this purpose, and for the ordination of the pastor elect, did not assemble till the 10th of December following. It is not improbable that this delay was caused by the interruptions produced that year by French and Indian hostilities. War was formally declared by England against France in 1756; but, for many months previous, military operations had been carried on by the respective Colonies of the two nations on this side of the Atlantic. In 1755 occurred Braddock's celebrated defeat. In the same year, hostile Indians, under the guidance of Canadian-French officers, menaced for the last time the frontier settlements of Massachusetts. They ravaged and burned towns in New Hampshire, on the Connecticut River. The inhabitants of Winchendon (then called Ipswich-Canada) asked the General Court for aid and protection; stating that Indians were about, so that they could not cultivate their fields, and were dependent on Lunenburg, Lancaster, and Groton, for food. In the month of August, 1755, a scouting party of soldiers discovered traces of hostile Indians in Winchendon. A fort was built, probably during the summer of 1755, in this township, for safety in case of an Indian attack.* While the homes and families of our first settlers were in such danger, it is not surprising that they postponed for a few months the completion of their church affairs and the ordination of the pastor. The dangers having at length ceased, an ecclesiastical council was assembled on the 10th of December, 1755, who, according to the certificate of the moderator recorded in the proprietors' records, "did gather a church, set apart and ordain the Rev. Daniel Pond the first minister of that plantation." † And thus, in conformity to their own liberties and conscientious

---

* The proprietors, at their meeting in October, 1755, voted "to make a reasonable allowance" to the persons who built the fort. I have not been able to ascertain its location. Probably it consisted of simple ramparts of logs and earth, within which any settlers might retire upon an alarm; and was thought defensible against a savage enemy, armed only with muskets.

† Mr. Pond was entitled, by the terms of his settlement, to have the original lot or right of land reserved, in the grant by the Legislature, for the first minister,— equal to a hundred and twenty-third part of the whole township; also fifty-five pounds of lawful money as "a settlement;" and a salary, for the first three years, of fifty-five pounds a year, and subsequently of fifty-two pounds a year.

judgment, and with the sympathy and fellowship of other churches, was organized this, the First Congregational Church of Christ in the town. The church assumed at its formation no sectarian or party name: it never has from that day to this. On the basis of Protestant Christianity, and of the simple, free, and scriptural usages and forms of the Congregational order and discipline, it stands, and has ever stood, calling no man master; because one is its Master, even Christ, and the members are all brethren.

Those twelve men, who, on that eventful day, acknowledged their signatures and the consent of their hearts to that church-organization, must have felt that they were then, indeed, laying "the foundations of many generations." I have before me the original paper, subscribed in the handwriting of each of the twelve. Precious relic! May it be safely preserved many centuries more!

The names of these twelve original founders are Daniel Pond, Joshua Hyde, Josiah Wheat, David Clark, Charles Baker, David Goddard, Jacob Byam, Phineas Byam, Zaccheus Barrett, Elias Wilder, Thomas Drury, John Chamberlin.

This original church-covenant conformed in its phraseology to the usual theology of the times. It was not drawn up, however, by Mr. Pond, or by any of the members, here; for it was the same as the one adopted, several years before, at the formation of the First Church in Athol, and which continued to be used there so lately as to the end of the venerable Mr. Esterbrook's life. Probably, in both cases, it was copied from some form in use elsewhere. Afterwards, Rev. Mr. Sparhawk substituted another form, — shorter, but of the same practical import, and less particular in its doctrinal expressions.

That was a great day for the inhabitants of Narraganset No. 6, a hundred years ago, which witnessed the first consecration of their public religious institutions. Friends, relatives, and strangers came in on horseback, from many miles, in large numbers. The meeting-house, then just erected, was crowded with people from far and near. A generous hospitality was afforded to all comers. The entertainment for the council, and the many guests from abroad, was made by Mr. Jason Whitney. The proprietors' ancient records contain the items of the provisions furnished on the occasion, and paid for out of their treasury, with the prices for the same: they were ample and generous. It is worthy of note, that there was no tea or coffee; but there was a barrel of cider, and liquors, according to the fashion of the times, in moderate quantities. Large kettles were scarce: one or two of brass were transported, at considerable expense, from other towns. Some provender for the horses, and other stores, had been brought from abroad. Among the items of food were fifty pounds of veal, at two cents and a quarter per pound; thirty-seven pounds and a half of pork, at four cents and a half; twenty-five pounds of beef, at two cents and three-quarters; "two geese and four hens," which cost together less than did six pounds of sugar. The price paid out of the treasury for horse-keeping was at the rate of nine cents a day each. To the inhabitants, it was a day of festivity and cheerful anticipations: they were manifesting their settled conviction, that the things of religion must be recognized as indispensable to the prosperity of the infant settlement, and their desire that gospel-institutions should strengthen and grow with the growth and strength of the town. They had called in the ministers and people of the neighboring towns for counsel, sympathy, and aid; and there, under the impressive circumstances and amid the primeval forest, did they invoke the blessing of God on those consecrations for which the day had been set apart.

But Mr. Pond's ministry, as already stated, was very short. In the course of three or four years, difficulties had arisen. A mutual council was called in to give its advice. They investigated and deliberated for two days. It was considered no light thing for minister and people to be separated. But the council, on the whole, gave their judgment in favor of his dismission. With this advice, both the minister and the proprietors complied. He ceased to preach here in August, 1759.

Mr. Pond, according to the best information I have been able to obtain, was born May 13, 1724, probably in Wrentham, Mass. He was graduated at Harvard University, Cambridge, in 1745, in the class with Gov. James Bowdoin. He did not continue in the ministry, but went to West Medway, then a part of Wrentham, and was a teacher, receiving students into his house. After Rev. Mr. Sparhawk's settlement here, Mr. Pond was dismissed from membership in this church, and recommended to the church in that place, to which he was received as a member, June, 1764. He seems to have enjoyed confidence and respect from the citizens there. He was very strongly opposed to what were called the Hopkinsian views in theology; and, upon the settlement of a minister in West Medway who advocated those views, he withdrew from that church to another, and, by the action he took, became the leader in a dissension in that town, which lasted many years. It is said that he finally removed to Otter Creek, and died there.

At the same meeting of proprietors at which the action of the council, in favor of dismissing Mr. Pond, was ratified, they chose Mr. Jonas Wilder, Rev. Aaron Whitney (of Petersham), and Mr. Daniel Knowlton, a committee to provide preaching in the township, with a view to another settlement. The first minister who came (September, 1759) was Mr. Josiah Brown,* who preached only three or four Sundays. He was followed by Mr. Francis Gardner, who seems to have been quite acceptable to the people; for he preached here at different times the greater part of a year. There were four or five other candidates before Mr. Sparhawk came; but Mr. Gardner supplied more Sundays than all the others.

---

* Perhaps Josiah Brown, graduate of Harvard College in 1735, who was never ordained.

Mr. Gardner was son of Rev. John Gardner, of Stowe; and born Feb. 17, 1736; graduated at Harvard College in 1755; and was ordained at Leominster, Dec. 22, 1762. He died June 4, 1814. His brother, Henry, was the first Treasurer of Massachusetts after the commencement of the Revolution, and was grandfather of the present Governor of the Commonwealth.

Mr. Gardner not proving to be the one who was to become the spiritual guide of the little flock here, their attention was turned to others. Mr. Thomas Rice preached the next largest number of Sundays. He was from Sutton, about twenty-five years old, and had been out of college three or four years. He was never ordained, but became a physician; and at length filled the office of Judge of the Court of Common Pleas, and other public posts, in Maine. Next came Mr. Lemuel Hedge, just from college; born in Hardwick; and finally settled as the minister of Warwick (then called Roxbury-Canada), Dec. 3, 1760, where he died Oct. 17, 1777. He was father of Professor Hedge, of Harvard University. There was also a "Rev. Mr. Jones, of Woburn," who preached a short time, perhaps only a single sabbath; * and a Mr. Whitney, for two sabbaths.†

Another of the young preachers employed was Stephen Shattuck, jun.; a classmate with Mr. Sparhawk at Harvard College. He was born in Littleton,

---

* Probably Rev. Cornelius Jones (H. C. 1752), the first minister in Rowe, Mass.

† Probably Rev. P. Whitney (H. C. 1759), afterwards minister of Shirley.

of which town his father was the first minister; and was brother of Dr. Benjamin Shattuck, the first physician of this town. Mr. Shattuck was never ordained. He kept school occasionally. His death took place in Littleton, in 1799.

The last candidate, before Mr. Sparhawk, was Mr. Thomas Fessenden, of Cambridge, then only twenty-two years old. He was graduated at Harvard College in 1758, at the age of nineteen; and was ordained at Walpole, N.H., Jan. 7, 1767, where he died in 1813.

In 1760 and 1761, the proprietors appointed on their committees, to supply the pulpit, Jonas Wilder, Charles Baker, Ebenezer Wright, and Zaccheus Barrett. By them, Mr. Ebenezer Sparhawk was introduced here; preaching in this place, for the first time, Nov. 29, 1760. The tradition remains, that, on the first journey hither, — coming on Saturday from Rutland, probably by way of Barre, on horseback, guided only by marked trees, — Mr. Sparhawk lost his way; and night coming on, and no habitations discernible, he was obliged to fasten his horse to a tree, and, as the weather was quite cold, was constrained, for safety, to walk in a circle about the tree all night. When morning came, the spot proved to be but a short distance from the house of Deacon Wilder, on the farm now owned by Col. George W. Sawyer. Mr. Sparhawk preached here through the greater part of the year 1761. One reason why the settlements of those days were more permanent than modern ones was, that candidates and parishes took time enough to become acquainted, and ascertain whether there was a mutual adaptation, before it was ventured to propose or accept a call.

Mr. Sparhawk received his call to settle here in July, accepted it in October, and was ordained Nov. 18, 1761. Many of the present congregation associate his manly form and dignified yet courteous bearing with the most hallowed of their early recollections. His memory is reverenced by all as that of a truly honest, pious, faithful minister of God. His settlement here in the freshness of youth, at the age of only twenty-three, remaining as he did till his death at almost threescore and ten, was a most happy thing for the town; for it was his ministry and influence, as already said, that gave character, in a great measure, to the first half-century of our church history. Nor has that influence ceased with his life: it has been felt for good to this day.

Mr. Sparhawk was born in that part of Cambridge which is now Brighton, June 15, 1738, of pious and respectable parents. He was instructed in the languages and fitted for college chiefly by Mr. Jonathan Winchester, of Brookline, who was afterwards minister of Ashburnham. He entered Harvard College, at Cambridge, at the age of fourteen years; and was graduated at eighteen, in the year 1756, the next year after the graduation of John Adams, second President of the United States. After leaving college, Mr. Sparhawk taught school in Lexington, Rutland, Shrewsbury, and Worcester. While teaching, he pursued his studies for the ministry; in part under the direction of the

Rev. Mr. Buckminster, of Rutland, the grandfather of the celebrated and beloved Joseph Stevens Buckminster, who was pastor of the Brattle-street Church in Boston. Mr. Sparhawk preached his first sermon at Charlestown, Jan. 20, 1760; and preached here upwards of thirty Sundays, in 1761, before his ordination. The council assembled for his settlement consisted of the representatives of seven churches, and was composed of six pastors and ten delegates. They met at the house of Mr. Zaccheus Barrett, where Mr. Sparhawk then boarded, — the house now occupied by the Dolbear family, Mr. Barrett's desendants, and which is said to have been the first *framed* house ever erected within the present bounds of the town. The public services of the ordination were conducted as follows: Introductory prayer by Rev. Mr. Davis, of Holden; charge by Rev. Mr. Hill, of Shutesbury; prayer "after the charge" by Rev. Mr. Maccarty, of Worcester; right hand of fellowship by Rev. Aaron Whitney, of Petersham. The sermon was preached by Rev. Joseph Buckminster, of Rutland, and was afterwards printed. I have been so fortunate as to obtain, in a distant town, a copy of that sermon, which is now before me. It is entire, with the exception of a single missing leaf; and, from the context, the connection of the absent passage is sufficiently evident. The text is 2 Thess. iii. 1; and the general theme of the discourse is the office of ministers of the gospel, and their need of their people's sympathy and prayers. It is an able, sensible, and practical discourse.

There is not a word in it which we should not now cordially accept.*

Mr. Sparhawk was settled upon an annual salary of £66. 13*s.* 4*d.*, which was equal to $222.22; with the amount of two years' salary additional, paid as "a settlement." This "settlement" money he invested in land. It was probably nearly or quite sufficient for the purchase of his farm of eighty acres, without buildings. It was stipulated that he should have leave to be absent three Sundays a year. This salary of two hundred and twenty-two dollars continued the same throughout his life. Small as such a support now seems, it was then considered by all a generous sum. It was probably, at the time of his ordination, more valuable — relatively to the prices of things, and the requisitions of a minister's living — than any of the salaries now paid by any of the religious societies in this town; and so continued for a great many years, with the exception of a portion of the troubled times of the Revolutionary War. At that time, the rate of wages for able-bodied men, doing long days' work and boarding themselves, was less than fifty cents a day. Thirty years later, the wages of carpenters and painters in this town were only four shillings a day, boarding themselves. Female help was less than fifty cents a week. The work of a pair of oxen was, for a long time, twenty-five cents a day. On the other hand, some articles, especially of foreign produce, were higher than

---

* See Appendix D.

now. The increase of expenses of living began to be materially felt chiefly within the ten or fifteen years before the close of his ministry; and the salary finally became quite inadequate. There seems to have been a want of justice on the part of the people, in the last ten years, in not consenting to increase it. A small addition for his firewood was voted for three years, from 1794 to 1797; but even this was not continued afterward. On the whole, it is probable, that, at the termination of the first half-century, the necessary expenses of living had about doubled, in the aggregate, from what they were at the beginning.*

About two years after his ordination, Mr. Sparhawk married Miss Abigail Stearns, daughter of Rev. David and Mrs. Ruth Stearns, of Lunenburg. She was about his own age. Her mother, on being afterward left a widow, married the Rev. Aaron Whitney, of Petersham. Mr. Sparhawk, having bought his farm, built, in 1764, the house which he inhabited more than forty years, till his death, and in which my colleague, who purchased it of his heirs, has resided for a still longer time. There were four sons born of Mr. Sparhawk's first marriage, one of whom died in infancy. Mrs. Ruth Sparhawk, his "valuable and beloved consort," as he called her, died of a fever, April 21, 1772. He was married again, to Miss Naomi Hill, daughter of Rev. Abraham and Naomi Hill, of Shutesbury.

---

* See Appendix E.

She was born Aug. 17, 1749, and survived her husband twenty-three years; dying in this town at the age of almost eighty, having enjoyed esteem and respect from the people. Of the second marriage, there were four sons and four daughters. Of Mr. Sparhawk's twelve children, only one died young. One son and three daughters still survive.

During forty-four years did Rev. Mr. Sparhawk faithfully and vigorously discharge his duties as minister of this people. At times, he had trials to bear in the duties of his office, and opposition to confront: but his dignity of character, his prudence, his firmness, perseverance, and conscientiousness, carried him through it all; and he enjoyed, in the last twenty years of his ministry, the respect and confidence of some who had before, sometimes not on good grounds, strongly opposed him. The last quarter-part of his ministry seems to have been passed in almost unbroken harmony with his people, with the exception of a very few persons, who also were inclined to signify their discontent with his successor.

The survey of our church history would be quite incomplete, were we not to include some account of the divisions and differences above referred to, which arose near the commencement of the Revolutionary War. I have devoted much time to the investigation of their causes and results, by means of the records of the parish as well as the church, and other sources of information. The conclusion, to my mind, is irresistible, that Rev. Mr. Sparhawk was thoroughly conscientious in the action he took; though in one or two important points he rested upon views, as to the rights of the churches, which were then held, indeed, by many ministers, but which are *now* discarded by all, and which, it seems probable, he himself later in life abandoned. The opposition to his cause was, in part, factious. There were those who found fault, without candor or reason, or sense of common justice. There were others, who, in a better spirit, considered themselves bound to resist his course as derogatory to the liberties of the churches, and inconsistent with our Congregational principles. At the same time, it is evident, from a careful study of the documents, that, except in the matters in which Mr. Sparhawk was acting upon the convictions referred to, his ministry met with no valid reproach. The frivolous character of the complaints brought forward in any other direction, even when the authors were in the height of controversy, show conclusively that his character and work were such as might endure even the scrutiny of enemies.

In explanation, it is to be noted that he was strict and faithful in his administration of church discipline. With the change of the times, this is now far less important, relatively, in regard to the tone of morals in the community, than it was in the early periods of the country. Every thing was then in a transition or forming state. It is, clear, that the decided stand taken in those days by pastors and churches, and enforced by requisition of confessions and by suspensions and exclusions, had a most material influence towards saving the New-England population — both the members of the churches, and those who were not so — from the peculiar liabilities to habits of immorality to which they were exposed by the circumstances and hardships of the early settlements. The method pursued in regard to the intercourse of churches with each other was also adapted, at that time, to secure good order and the purity of the ministry. The few cases of discipline in this church, during Mr. Sparhawk's ministry, for personal immorality, seem to have been judiciously and impartially conducted, and salutary in their effect. But the pastor felt it a duty to withhold church fellowship from persons, who, without conformity to established usages, withdrew from communion, or who had been connected with unjustifiable schisms in their towns, or violent and irregular dismissions of the settled pastors. The application Mr. Sparhawk made of these principles to a celebrated controversy, arising in the town of Bolton, was also the occasion of developing his views of the prerogatives of a pastor, and especially of asserting, on his part, a supposed right to veto the decisions of the church. By this means, he was brought into a serious controversy with a majority of his church and people, who stood up for ecclesiastical freedom as they were also standing for civil liberty. In this they were right, though they did not all behave in a good spirit. A division had taken place in Bolton, and Mr. Sparhawk considered one of the parties disorderly and schismatic. He was unwilling that a person adhering to that party should have fellowship and communion here. But this church, after deliberate and protracted investigation in reference to the case of receiving such a person, voted contrary to their pastor's views, by a majority of two-thirds. Mr. Sparhawk declared his *non-concurrence*, which he considered equal to a veto. This was not admitted. He was, however, resolute in his position, and even went so far as to direct the deacons not to administer the sacrament to the person from Bolton, whom the church had voted at liberty to partake.*

The greater part of the members were unwilling actually to press the controversy to the point of separation of minister and people. In that result it would have ended, had there not been, on the part of the majority, a spirit of conciliation; for Mr. Sparhawk was evidently prepared to undergo any trial or sacrifice whatever, rather than yield what he considered a pastor's sacred prerogative and duty, — to veto decisions of his church which he deemed wrong. Had those who differed from him insisted upon carrying out their views, it is certain he would have demanded a dismission. A great majority of the ministers of the Commonwealth at that time agreed with him. Prominent among those who held that a pastor's dissenting from a vote of a church rendered that vote a nullity, were the Rev. Zabdiel Adams, of

---

* About a year and a half afterwards, the church voted, by a majority, to rescind their original vote.

Lunenburg; and Rev. Mr. Mellen, of Sterling. The latter person practised in his own church, in regard to the Bolton case, on precisely the same ground as Mr. Sparhawk did here. He was dismissed in consequence. The Ecclesiastical Council, convoked here in 1780 to advise the church and pastor, sustained his position, as a matter of privilege in his office. Increase Mather wrote in favor of the idea, that pastors hold this power of a negative voice. On the other hand, President Stiles, of Yale College, and others, declared against it.*

The question that had been brought into issue was indeed a vital one for the religious freedom of New England; but it is instructive to see how much better a principle of truth and right is vindicated by the calm and patient appeal to reason and conscience, and the waiting, if need be, for the judgment of posterity, than by angry contest. The fathers here were satisfied they were right on this point. They knew it was a most important issue for our congregational liberties; but they also knew that Mr. Sparhawk was sincere in his opposite opinion. It would have been easy to have made a division in the church and town, and had a harsh controversy kept up for long years. There were some in the church and parish so disposed; but the majority in both wisely determined,

---

* In 1782, the parties in Bolton were re-united; and, in 1783, this church by vote expressed their disposition not to postpone communion any longer with any part of that church, and to express fellowship with its members without exception. In 1785, Rev. Phineas Wright was ordained pastor of the whole body there. This church attended in the council.

that, while they would retain their opinion, Mr. Sparhawk should also enjoy his. And what was the result? About twenty years afterward, as the records indicate, Mr. Sparhawk himself, probably by a change in his own views gradually wrought out, fully recognized the church's independent right of action; and now, when another generation has made its calm review, there is nowhere any church or minister in the whole Congregational body, in either of its two great branches, that admits any such prerogative in a pastor! In this respect, the just and scriptural principles of our liberty have fully prevailed.

May we not believe that other important questions now at issue among the churches, and their discussion, too often attended with ill-temper and division, will, in another generation, be settled with equal unanimity and truth? Though Mr. Sparhawk was acting upon a mistaken theory, there can be no doubt that he regarded his course as a painful duty. For that loyalty to his own convictions he deserved to be honored. The same steadfastness of principle which made him confront so decided an opposition among his people, also made him, in other things, a faithful minister and a reliable man. Some, however, continued dissatisfied. A number of members absented themselves from the communion for a year or two. This difficulty appears to have chiefly subsided in the course of the years 1779 and 1780. Meanwhile, however, there was a disposition in the parish to manifest opposition. One of the most effectual grounds for the discontented to take at that day, if plausibility could be given to it, would be to assert that the minister was not friendly to the cause of the American Revolution. This course they took. There seems to have been little foundation for it. No doubt, Mr. Sparhawk had a wider view, than some of the people, of the great difficulties and dangers that must be encountered by the feeble Colonies in undertaking to resist the mighty power of Great Britain. He was not ready to encourage every violent speech, and favor any rash enterprise that might be suggested, in the revolutionary affairs. Some of his most intimate associates in the ministry felt rather favorable to the cause of the king. But there is no evidence that he was not friendly to the cause of liberty, and desirous of the success of the Revolution. In 1774, a fast had been recommended in reference to the civil troubles. For some reason, Mr. Sparhawk made no appointment to observe it. The town chose a committee "to treat with him on account of the uneasiness about not having a fast." The result seems to have been satisfactory, though it cannot now be ascertained what the grounds were. He was accustomed in his public devotions to pray for the king, and continued to do so after hostilities had begun. Some of the people waited upon him to remonstrate. One may fancy the quiet satisfaction with which he invited these gentlemen, a few months after, to come to his house and *advise him;* "for," said he, "I find myself in a difficulty. You complained of me, and said a patriotic minister ought not to offer public prayers for King George III.; and now I have received a circular from the American Congress, requesting all clergymen to offer prayers on the sabbath in behalf of the king and his government, and that the Almighty may help them to come to a better mind. What shall I do, brethren?" Of course, they had to allow that the recommendation of the Congress ought to be complied with. During a period of two or three years, there was a considerable disposition in the parish to withhold suitable pecuniary support; that is, they offered payment only in the depreciated continental paper-money. From 1777 to 1780, the paper-money being a legal currency, the nominal prices of every thing were enormously inflated. They granted each year only the amount of the regular salary; which, being payable in this paper-money, he refrained from accepting. In 1778, he proposed to graduate the amount of salary according to the scale of prices as they stood before the war. The parish declined; but a subscription was made by individuals towards his support. But, in 1779, they voted, on articles, to see whether the parish would provide for his "honorable and decent support as a gospel minister;" that his salary for the year *previous* should be six hundred pounds; and that, for the year ensuing, — the paper-money having further depreciated, — it should be twelve hundred pounds (equal to four thousand dollars). Even this, however, did not cover the rapidly advancing depreciation. These votes were all passed by very small majorities. In 1780, they declined to make additional compensation. A precinct meeting was warned with articles to hear and take into consideration any complaints on the part of either minister or people. This being intended to include some of the differences arising out of the votes passed in the *church*, Mr. Sparhawk declined to attend, on the ground that an ecclesiastical council was the only proper tribunal. Such a council had already been invited by letters missive from the pastor and the church, and assembled June 7, 1780. They justified Mr. Sparhawk, and sanctioned the votes of the church.* The parish, by votes at different times, manifested their unwillingness to have Mr. Sparhawk leave them; and the council advised against it, provided suitable provision should be made for his support. He had declined taking any of the continental bills for salary; and they now ceased to pass as currency at any price. His salary was in arrears for five years. At length, in the beginning of 1782, he commenced an action at law "against the First Precinct in Templeton" for the same. They made an amicable settlement, and promptly paid the whole, with interest, in compliance with his terms, with the exception of a hundred and sixty dollars, which he had offered to give up, as he said, "for the ease and relief of those less able to pay taxes;" and, "as I have ever been kind to this people, still to approve myself so," — the sum to

---

* See Appendix F.

be allowed, according to the discretion of the assessors, as deduction from particular individuals' taxes. It was also made by Mr. Sparhawk a condition of this settlement, that the precinct should, the same week, pay to the attorney and sheriff all costs and charges, and bring their receipt. Thus the affair ended. Against the vote of the parish in his favor, in 1779, a number of voters expressly recorded their dissent; and eight of them filed a written protest, assigning their reasons, and declaring, that, in their opinion, it "would be more to the honor of God and religion for the minister and people to separate, unless there may be a speedy settlement between them." The reasons assigned in this protest for their dissatisfaction are thoroughly frivolous. It was mainly the old story, which has been so many times repeated in all ages, of persons who had commenced and carried on controversy in a bitter and violent spirit turning about, and charging the other party, on trifling grounds, with showing a want of Christian meekness and forbearance. The ministry of Mr. Sparhawk continued nearly twenty-five years after these difficulties were disposed of; and we hear no more of these contentions. Most of the dissenters continued under his ministry; and some, at least, seemed to have been cordially attached to him to the end of life. Some, however, among whom was the probable author of the written protest referred to, became active in establishing a Baptist society in the town, which was organized shortly after.

The formation of a Baptist church in this town, and the withdrawal to it of a number of the members of the First Church, was regarded by Mr. Sparhawk as a serious trial. Undoubtedly his uneasiness was not so much on account of their deviating from *his* views, as because they made it a ground of division and separation. The whole number of members who withdrew from this to the Baptist church during Mr. Sparhawk's ministry was seventeen, — ten men and seven women. They were not "dismissed and recommended," though some of them had requested it: but this was on the ground, that the Baptist churches refused to hold communion with the Congregationalist churches, and that this church desired not "to trouble any society with a letter of dismission which was probably indisposed to have special fellowship with this church;" * and also on the ground, often reiterated by Mr. Sparhawk, that the convictions any member might have on the subject of baptism were no proper reason for a separation from it, "because those of this church are free and willing that any of the members of it should satisfy their consciences in regard to that matter;" † "and the church does not require of them, to the continuance of their communion, any thing contrary to their present judgment." ‡ But though not "dismissing and recommending" these members, in the techni-

* Church Records, vol. i. p. 74. † Ibid. vol. i. p. 243.
‡ Ibid. vol. i. p. 78.

cal sense, the church many times voted its willingness to give certificates of character and regular standing, accompanied with declaration, on the part of the church, of its full adherence to the principles of the right of private judgment, and liberty of conscience. By this they meant liberty to withdraw from the church, as well as liberty while remaining in it. Those whose persuasions led them to the Baptist denomination, therefore, quietly withdrew without censure. Votes to this effect were passed in 1787, and were renewed at various times, especially in 1793, in answer to a request from Samuel Fisk, who had become a Baptist, and desired, that, "as he differed from them in some points of religion, he might be dismissed." On this application, it was voted, "That the pastor signify to whom it may concern, that he is in regular standing with this church, and that they are disposed, on occasion, to recommend him accordingly; and also signify that it is the sense and mind of the church, every person has a right to private judgment, and liberty of conscience." * No narrower ground has ever been occupied by this church. Its free consent, as a permanent standing rule, to all such withdrawals for conscience' sake, was, upon deliberate consideration, affirmed again nearly forty years afterward, — in 1832.†

Looking back to the personal ministrations of Mr. Sparhawk for so long a period, — comprehend-

---

* Church Records, vol. i. p. 239.

† Records, vol. ii.; report of committee, and subsequent votes.

ing as they did the time when the institutions and character of our town were forming, and taking their tone, — how impressive is the contemplation! We may imagine those scenes. We may depict to our thoughts that congregation which assembled so regularly, summer and winter, in that first house of wor ship, with no spire, or bell sounding its invitations, and which was never warmed in the coldest season; a bare shelter, with scarcely any attempt at adornment, or impression upon the feelings from any source, save by the simple majesty and sacredness of the idea of the public worship of the Almighty on his hallowed day, and by the truths uttered in the services. In the earlier days, the assembly consisted mostly of the young and middle-aged: for the first settlers, very many of them, *commenced* their homes and the business of life here; and so, for some years, there were few old persons among them. They had but little store of this world's goods. They made no pretensions to elegance of style or dress. They were robust, hardy men and women, who knew the difficulties of the wilderness, and were not afraid to encounter them. Into that humble edifice came — a large portion from distances of two, three, or more miles — such a congregation on each sabbath morning. They enter at doors on three sides of the house, and take their places, not in pews, for the most part, but in long seats which occupied the central spaces below for many years, and the galleries almost wholly, as long as the house stood. The men sit together on the west side; the women, together on the east. The singers, for the first quarter of a century, it seems, were accustomed to sit below, in the seats opposite the pulpit, toward the south (that is, the front) door. Not till after this space in the body of the house below came to be fully occupied with pews, did the singers, in 1785, resort to the gallery; at least, such is the only inference now to be drawn. The people — those who do not occupy pews — are seated both below and in the galleries, according to an order of precedence prescribed by a committee of the town, — the seats most eligible, or considered most dignified, being occupied by those taxed for the most property; and so through the whole, in a nicely graduated order. So much deference did the fathers seem to pay to distinctions of worldly prosperity, even in the house of God. And yet, perhaps, it was not quite that; for as good order was thought to require some rule, and some permanency of place for each one, they might adopt that standard of preference simply for want of any better. At least, they knew well, and felt it in their inmost souls, that, before the great Being whom they came to worship, all were equal; that he looked down upon them with no distinctions save of character. They deemed the disciples of Christ possessed all of equal prerogative in things of religion and ecclesiastical order. No decision of pope or bishop or presbytery had such weight in their minds as the simple vote of the brethren in church-meeting expressed, attended with no form or ceremony; and, because their Bible had taught them these doctrines, it had also made them free as citizens, never to be subjected to any usurping tyranny of king or parliament. Such was the congregation. When assembled, their good pastor comes to meet them. He is clad in the professional garb of the times; always, as long as he lived, wearing the ancient "small-clothes," with bright silver knee-buckles, and the three-cornered clerical hat. He was of middle stature; his appearance, in the latter part of life at least, striking by reason of his flowing locks, which combined with his general bearing and his dress to impart a peculiarly venerable aspect. He enters the pulpit, and conducts the sacred service mainly according to usages of the present time. The psalm or hymn is sung without accompaniment of any musical instruments; which, it seems, were not employed here till near the close of Mr. Sparhawk's life. He reads a portion of Scripture. Prayers are offered. The sermon is preached: usually, beyond doubt, it was well written, sensible, not largely imaginative or dealing much with metaphors and comparisons, practical rather than speculative,* and delivered with dignity and quiet earnestness, with deliberate, perhaps somewhat slow, utterance. When the benediction was pronounced, the whole congregation waited quietly in their places till the minister had passed out of the house.

---

* Not many of his writings were printed. A discourse preached Jan. 18, 1794, at the funeral of Dr. Benjamin Shattuck, was published, and a charge given at the ordination of Rev. Mr. Esterbrook at Athol.

Upon those ministrations of religion the divine blessing rested. Within the walls of that weather-beaten sanctuary, genuine songs of praise were offered and devout prayers addressed to the Father of all. There parents brought their infants, as a general custom; desiring to obtain for them, by the rite of baptism, according to the notions of the time, some special impartation of divine grace. And, by that act of consecration of their offspring to God, the parents' hearts were truly moved with an increased sensibility to the things of religion, and their duties in the Christian nurture of the children. There the Lord's Supper was administered with its tender and hallowed associations. In all the observances, liberal, enlightened, and practical views of Christianity and of personal duty prevailed. But a change came. Before infirmities of advanced age should overcome him, the pastor was called away from his earthly charge. Mr. Sparhawk died at the age of sixty-seven, of apoplexy, Nov. 25, 1805, after a brief illness, lasting only from Thursday to the Monday following. The sermon at his funeral was preached by the Rev. Dr. Payson, of Rindge, a member of the Association of Ministers.

During his ministry of forty-four years, Mr. Sparhawk received to this church, by profession, two hundred and forty-five persons, — a hundred men and a hundred and forty-five women; also, by letters of dismission and recommendation, from other churches, fifty-three persons, — nineteen men and thirty-four women. A number of the members lived within the territory of Phillipston. Twenty-five persons were dismissed from this church to form that one. It is worthy of remark, that almost the whole of the two hundred and forty-five members, received upon profession, had been baptized here or elsewhere in their infancy. I think that Mr. Sparhawk in his whole life did not baptize more than ten adults. He baptized more than a thousand infants.

Mr. Sparhawk usually enjoyed good health, though he was never of strong constitution. He was a person of warm friendships and a generous hospitality. He was a good and correct scholar. He had a ready and accurate memory. It is evident, by many considerations, that he was superior in mind and education to many or most ministers of his day in this neighborhood. While he maintained a sort of official dignity, which perhaps kept young persons especially at too great distance, yet, upon acquaintance, he was courteous and affable. He was a *good man* from *principle.* He was conscientious in his house, in his parish, and in the pulpit. Pious and faithful in his ministry, he passed, we trust, to receive the reward on high.

After Mr. Sparhawk's death, the church made choice of Rev. Ezekiel Bascom, who was pastor at Phillipston (then called Gerry), to act as its moderator till the settlement of another pastor. Deacon Paul Kendall was also chosen assistant moderator and clerk. A special day of fasting and prayer, in consequence of his death, was appointed

February, 1806; and Rev. Messrs. Lee, Esterbrook, Bascom, and Osgood were invited to attend. Only a few preachers, except the neighboring pastors, supplied here during the vacancy. Rev. Mr. Grovesnor, a man about sixty years old, who was settled in Paxton, in this county, and elsewhere, preached for a time. It is believed there were but three who were considered as "candidates;" namely, Messrs. Fisher, Ritchie, and Wellington. The first (Mr. Jesse Fisher) was a native of Wendell, Mass., and a graduate of Harvard College in the class of 1803. He was for some time teacher in the New-Salem Academy, and was ordained and settled in Connecticut. He died in 1836. The second (Mr. William Ritchie) was a graduate of Dartmouth College in the class of 1804. He was settled as pastor of the First Parish in Needham, where he had a long and useful ministry. Both these studied for the ministry with Rev. Dr. Lathrop, of Springfield. No vote was taken here in regard to the settlement of either of them.

Nov. 17, 1806, the parish and the church concurred, with scarcely a dissenting voice, in the choice of Mr. Charles Wellington as their pastor. They proposed a salary of five hundred dollars per annum; and the amount of one year's salary additional, by way of "settlement." This was considered a liberal support, according to the standard of the time. Still, on account of the increase of prices and enhanced cost of living generally, it was then probably little, if any, better than was originally the support voted for Mr. Sparhawk at the time of his settlement.

Mr. Wellington's ordination took place Feb. 25, 1807. A council of nine churches, pastors and delegates, assembled at the house of Deacon Paul Kendall, where Mr. Wellington at first boarded. Rev. Dr. Cushing, of Waltham, was moderator; Rev. Festus Foster, of Petersham, scribe. The sermon was preached by Rev. Dr. Cushing, of Waltham; the prayer of ordination was offered by Rev. Samuel Kendall, D.D., of Weston; the charge was by Rev. Joseph Lee, of Royalston; the right hand of fellowship by Rev. Joseph Esterbrook, of Athol; introductory and concluding prayers, by Rev. John Foster, of Brighton, and Rev. Jonathan Osgood, of Gardner. The other pastors present in council were Rev. E. L. Bascom and Rev. James Thompson. The service was concluded by singing Dr. Watts's version of the hundred and twenty-second psalm, —

"How pleased and blest was I," &c., —

which was read before pronouncing the benediction by the newly consecrated pastor.*

The town at that time contained between eleven and twelve hundred inhabitants. The old first meeting-house was still in use, though soon to be exchanged for the present one. Almost that whole generation has passed away. There are, indeed, a considerable number still in the congregation who remember that ordination-day; but the men and women of the time,

* He was born in Waltham, Feb. 20, 1780; graduated at Harvard College in the class of 1802; and received from that institution the honorary degree of Doctor of Divinity in 1854.

who bore active and responsible parts, have almost all gone. Only three or four of the communicants whom he first met here at the Lord's table survive; and only one still resides here, and retains her connection with this church. But the pastoral relation, that day formed, still continues; and, at the end of almost half a century, he who then became your minister is with you; his prayers are still offered up in the congregation, asking that as God was with the fathers, so he may be with the children. Still does he bear testimony to that cause of gospel truth and righteousness which he has so long and faithfully advocated among this people. This is not the fitting occasion to speak in detail of the characteristics and benefits of that ministry, which has covered almost the whole of the last half-century of the existence of this church. Many there are who treasure the record thereof in their hearts as a precious possession.

Not long after the time of the ordination, the parish voted to build a new meeting-house.* The *old* house was raised, July 3, 1753, in the presence of a large concourse, many of whom had come from Chockset, now Sterling. The vote to build it was

---

* The proceedings of the First Parish, as a legal corporation, from the beginning till now, are to be traced in the "Proprietors' Records," vol. i. up to August, 1754, vol. ii. up to the incorporation of the town in 1762; thence in the records of the town of Templeton, vol. i. till our territory in Phillipston was set off as a separate precinct in 1774; thence in the record-book of the first precinct (in the office of the town-clerk, and which was also used by the selectmen as a receipt-book), till the First Parish and town were again legally identified by the incorporation of "Gerry" in 1786; thence in the town-records again, vol. ii. till 1806, when the parish took an organization distinct from the town; and since, in the First-Parish Records.

passed by the proprietors, May 8, 1751; and a tax of sixteen shillings was laid on each original right of land in the township, for the purpose. An addition to this tax was afterwards made of four shillings more. A location was selected as early as 1743, perhaps before, probably by the committee chosen in 1734 to lay out the forty-acre lots. In 1752, the building committee were authorized to change the site within a distance "not exceeding forty rods, and still on the same original lot." The house stood a few rods south-eastwardly of the present one, fronting to the south, so that the front-door looked exactly in the direction of the road that leads from Rev. Dr. Wellington's house hither. The whole surrounding land, at the time of the erection of the first meeting-house, was covered with a heavy growth of wood and timber. The frame of the house was of *chestnut*, and was all cut — so the oldest member of this congregation has informed me — upon this common. When the house was built, there still were standing a number of large original trees so near as to have fallen upon it, had they been blown over. After the first minister was settled, a child, straying from the meeting, was "lost in the woods," on the common, one Sunday; and the whole congregation turned out to search for it. The work of building the meeting-house was undertaken by Mr. John Brooks, from Sterling. The timber was to be furnished by the proprietors, who also were to provide for the glazing, pulpit, &c. The whole cost in money, including the sums appropriated by the town a few years later "towards finishing it," was about two hundred and twenty-five pounds,—equal to seven hundred and fifty dollars.

In 1809, it was agreed to build the present meeting-house. Its dimensions are almost twice that of the former one; it being sixty-five feet in length, with projection of five feet for columns in front, fifty-five feet in width, and posts thirty-two feet. The committee for the purpose were Dr. Josiah Howe, Benjamin Read, Eden Baldwin, Leonard Stone, Deacon Jonathan Cutting, Jonathan Cutting, jun., and Joshua Richardson. The builders were Mr. Elias Carter, of Brimfield, and Mr. Jonathan Cutting, jun., of Templeton. The raising was commenced June 26, 1810; and the house was completed in September, 1811. The last service in the old house was held Sept. 1, 1811. It was agreed to devote the old building for the purpose of a town-house; and, being moved to the place where now stands the house of Mrs. Lydia Newton, it was so occupied for about thirty years. It was then taken down; and the timbers, being found in excellent preservation, now compose the frame of Mrs. Newton's house.

What sacred and impressive associations must there have been filling all minds on leaving the old house! "Those walls had resounded with all the varying notes of Christian worship." Within them, how many devout prayers had been offered, how many lessons of heavenly truth been inculcated! How many of a generation, then already nearly passed away, had there laid upon the altar of God the burden of their hearts, in affliction, in anxiety, in penitence, and also in faith, hope, and charity! In that house, too, had been transacted all the municipal affairs of the town from its incorporation. There the fathers, kindled with love for their ancient birthright of freedom, had met in solemn council on that tremendous question of resistance to the usurping attempts of their king. There they had passed those deliberate votes, expressing nothing more than the reality of their high and stern resolve, whereby they determined, that "if the Continental Congress should, for the safety of these United Colonies, declare them independent of the kingdom of Great Britain, we, the said inhabitants, do solemnly engage, with our lives and fortunes, to support them in the measure." * In that unadorned house of worship they had learned how they held their freedom, not by grant of Magna Charta, but by the will of God. There they had been taught, that piety toward him is the only sure foundation of justice and charity toward man. The day which witnessed the final parting from that ancient building as a temple of worship must indeed have been of most affecting interest. An appropriate discourse was preached by the then recently settled pastor, and was published together with his sermon at the dedication of the new house, which was Sept. 19, 1811. The enterprise of building it had been carried to very successful completion in all respects. Owing to the difference between that time and

---

* Town Records, vol. i. p. 201, May 24, 1776.

the present in the price of materials and labor, the cost was less than half of what it would be now. The whole was defrayed by sale of the pews. It is said, that, at the time, this was regarded as the best meeting-house in the county of Worcester. It certainly justified the commendation given in the dedication sermon in these words: "In this house we discover not a finical nicety: we discover a just proportion; we see a majestic simplicity; we see a simplicity blended with much elegance and beauty."

The public spirit of the people was further shown by the purchase at that time, by means of a parish-tax, of the first bell that ever called the people of the town to the house of God.* About this time, a new and active interest was felt in the subject of sacred music; and the choir here was long regarded as the best in this region. Singing-schools were provided, in part, as a parochial charge. Musical instruments were procured. In former times, great objections were felt by many to the use of instruments in the services of the sanctuary; it being imagined they were inconsistent with proper devotion. So late as 1797, it was a great satisfaction to Mr. Sparhawk, that, on the subject being brought up in a church meeting, no one voted for their introduction.† In 1804, however, the town voted "to have the bass-viol used in the meeting-

---

* Three others have been procured since by this parish, as successive defects occurred; namely, in 1815, 1829, and 1853.

† For nearly half a century, the choice of choristers, and other matters relating to singing, were determined by votes of the church.

house." The organ now used here was first opened in the autumn of 1832. Mr. Abel Sanger, of Warwick, a native of Templeton and an eminent musician, left by his will seven hundred dollars to this parish for the purchase of an organ; and the builder, Mr. William M. Goodrich, also a native of this place, generously, and to his honor, furnished for that sum the present instrument, though it was of the value of a thousand dollars.

Several different books of psalms and hymns have been used in the public devotions of this church. The first book, a century ago, was the Psalms of Sternhold and Hopkins. This was a version of the Hebrew Psalms, originally used three hundred years ago, in the beginning of the Protestant Reformation. It was introduced by royal authority into the English churches, in the reign of King Edward VI. Its lines are so rugged and uncouth, that it has been described by calling it "the songs of David *with the poetry taken out.*" Very few of these pieces are now thought worthy of use by any denomination. Yet the pioneers here, "in those words, no doubt, worthily uttered the praise of God." They loved it; and it was a sore trial to some of them * when the church voted, in 1762, to substitute Tate and Brady's Psalms, with Watts's Hymns. These psalms were also introduced into the English Established Church by royal authority. There is a plain, simple

* So I was informed by the late Mrs. Mary Dolbear, referring especially to her father, Z. Barrett.

majesty in many of them; but they are little used in modern collections. In 1791, Watts's Psalms were substituted for Tate and Brady's. This change also was not made without some difficulty. To Dr. Watts are the churches of Christ more indebted than to any other writer for their words of sacred song. There are, however, great differences of style and sentiment among his pieces: some of them have striking and serious defects. There are a few expressions in his book which seem to deserve the censure laid upon them by an eminent living clergyman of the church of England, when he calls them "shocking words, which change the glory of the incorruptible God into the likeness of a corruptible man." But notwithstanding any objections or defects noticeable in Watts's Psalms and Hymns, considered as the only book for the devotions of a congregation, still, in great part, they present an admirable combination of fervent piety with beauty and strength; and, as the poet Montgomery has said, "every sabbath, in every region of the earth where his native tongue is spoken, thousands and tens of thousands of voices are sending the sacrifices of prayer and praise to God, in the strains which he prepared for them more than a century ago."

Watts's Psalms and Hymns were exclusively used here till 1827, when my colleague prepared a pamphlet to be used with it, containing a selection of about a hundred additional hymns, many of them in metres not found in Watts. These hymns were of excellent character, and proved a valuable addition to the services. In 1839, the present collection of psalms and hymns was introduced. It was compiled by the late Rev. Dr. Greenwood, of Boston; and, with the best pieces of Watts and Doddridge, comprises also a wide range of authors, whose hymns had not before been accessible for use in the public services.

As already indicated, it is not my purpose, in these discourses, to go into much detail of the ministry in the second half-century of the church, which is occupied by the pastorate of my colleague. In several respects, it has noticeable coincidences with the ministry of Rev. Mr. Sparhawk. It was during the time from the twentieth to the thirtieth year of the last-named ministry that the secessions, before described, occurred; and it was exactly a quarter of a century after the present senior pastor's ordination — namely, in March, 1832 — that the first request was presented, signed by eleven members of the church, for dismission, "to be formed into a Trinitarian Congregational church." The church, fully recognizing the principles of liberty of conscience, voted to grant the request. Others soon after withdrew for the same purpose; the whole number of members who have been dismissed up to this time, to join the Trinitarian church, being twenty-eight. Of course, this secession could not but be a trial to the feelings of the pastor, who had been with them in so many sacred experiences for a quarter of a century; had ministered to them according to such light as, in his honest study of God's word, had been given to him. But, whatever the trial might have been to him, I believe that those who considered it a duty to withdraw never felt that they had occasion to complain of the spirit in which their former pastor met it. More recently, other societies also have been formed in the town.*

After a time, the failing health of the pastor began to interrupt the constancy of his public services. Temporary provision was made by the parish, at various times, for his aid in the pulpit, especially in the years 1839, 1840, and subsequently. In 1841, the settlement of a colleague was contemplated, and Rev. Daniel B. Parkhurst, a graduate of Yale College in the class of 1837, invited to preach as a candidate; but he declined to receive a call.

Rev. Mr. Wellington's health having become somewhat improved, he supplied a large part of the time till 1843; when, it being found that his health would not probably enable him to continue in the sole charge of the society, an arrangement was made, with great cordiality, by which it was understood that the parish would settle a colleague; that Mr. Wellington, being released from all responsibility for active service, should continue as senior pastor; and that his salary should cease, — a subscription, however, being made to pay him the sum of one thousand dollars. This arrangement having been completed, the parish voted, Oct. 4, 1843, to give a call to Mr. Edmund B. Willson † to settle as col-

---

* See APPENDIX G. † Now pastor at West Roxbury, Mass.

league pastor. This invitation was declined. A call was given, Jan. 2, 1844, to Mr. Norwood Damon, and accepted by him. He was ordained here Feb. 21, 1844. The sermon was preached by Rev. F. D. Huntington; the charge was by Rev. Alonzo Hill; the ordaining prayer was offered by Rev. N. Gage; and the address to the society was given by Rev. Dr. Thompson. Rev. Mr. Damon resigned his ministry, Nov. 1, 1845. The supply of the pulpit was then resumed by the senior pastor. During a part of the winter, he was assisted by several members of the Cambridge divinity-school class of 1846; * and afterward he preached most of the time till August of the same year. In November, a call was given to the present junior pastor; and my ordination as colleague took place Jan. 13, 1847, with the concurrence of a council of nine churches. The Scripture was read by the senior pastor; the sermon was preached by Rev. Calvin Lincoln, of Fitchburg; and the ordaining prayer offered by Rev. William H. White, of Littleton; — the charge being given by Rev. Dr. Thompson, of Barre; the right hand of fellowship by Rev. S. H. Winkley, of Boston; and the address to the society by Rev. Dr. Barrett, of Boston.

---

* They were Messrs. G. F. Clark, F. McIntire, L. J. Livermore, and E. G. Adams. Mr. Livermore (now pastor at Clinton) also preached, by invitation of the parish committee, soon after he left the theological school, but declined to receive a call here. These — with the other persons just named as officiating during Dr. Wellington's ill health, and those who have been before spoken of as preachers here previous to Mr. Sparhawk's ordination, or between his death and the ordination of the senior pastor — I believe to comprise *all* who, from the very first, were ever regarded as preaching in this parish in the capacity of "candidates for settlement."

A few weeks after that time, my colleague preached his fortieth anniversary discourse; and a kind Providence has granted that he should continue among his people to the close of the century, still officiating from time to time, as his strength would permit, in all the sacred ministrations of this house and of the pastoral office. In how many of your dwellings has his voice been heard in prayer for the household! To how many stricken hearts has he been a son of consolation! How many have received from him their early and lasting impressions of religious truth and duty! Almost the whole of those to whom he here first administered the Christian sacraments have already passed on to experience, in the spiritual world, the realities contemplated on earth only by faith. The number of members of this church who, between his ordination and the close of the century, have died in communion with it, is about one hundred and eighty-five.

Through this long term of my colleague's ministry, the customary succession of sacred services has been maintained. The unchanging message of the gospel has been delivered, yet in its ever-varying adaptation to the changing circumstances of the community and of individuals. During this time, the Sunday School — blessed instrument of Christian instruction and of spiritual influence — was established. It was commenced here in 1827. For the most part, its teachers have been exceedingly faithful, well qualified, and persevering. The Sunday-school Library has been instituted, and is well sustained by your annual contributions. It now contains upwards of a thousand volumes, and is a source of great good to the young.

Missionary associations have also been formed among us, to enable us to combine our interest, and unite our pecuniary aid, which has been bestowed in generous contributions, to assist in the great work and duty of promoting Christianity abroad.

The Ladies' Social Circle, under its present organization, was first formed in 1835; another organization for similar purposes having existed some years previously. The purpose of the Ladies' Circle is to furnish charitable assistance to the needy, promote the cause of Christianity by missionary aid and in other ways, to provide a library for the use of its members, and to encourage mutual acquaintance and sympathy. In the last respect, its meetings have been of great value. At its formation, it consisted of thirty-six members. The number was soon after much increased; and a general interest has constantly been manifested in it. The number has varied in different years; but, on an average, there have been about seventy members for each year. The funds raised by means of the annual assessments, and by the avails of their industry in the meetings, have amounted, during the period of the existence of the Ladies' Society (beside the garments, &c., given away), to somewhat over a thousand dollars. The number of volumes collected in their library is about six hundred.

As the century is closing, a substantial provision

is being made for the future by means of the commodious parsonage-house which the generosity of the people has just provided, and which is to remain as the possession of this parish so long as the conditions are fulfilled of supporting the Christian ministry. It will be a place, I trust, around which, as the permanent dwelling-place of successive ministers of the society, pleasant and sacred associations will long cluster. Let it be a place of free and happy resort. May it witness the unfolding of many a spiritual emotion and serious thought, and many a hallowed confidence in the pastor of the flock, even for generations to come!

Without dwelling further on instrumentalities employed or provisions made during the last half-century of our existence, I will proceed to a brief summary of the most important statistics of this church for the whole century.

As already noticed, there have been only two vacancies in the pastoral office, from the beginning, through the whole hundred years. Both together amounted to about three years and a half; viz., from August, 1759, to November, 1761, and from November, 1805, to February, 1807. The number of persons belonging to the church, in all, has been five hundred and ninety-eight, — two hundred and nineteen men and three hundred and seventy-nine women. Of these, ninety-one were received upon recommendation from other churches; the remainder, by profession. The largest number received in any one year, by profession, was twenty-five; namely, in

1811. In the respective periods, the members becoming connected with the church were as follows: Original founders, before Mr. Pond's ordination, twelve men; during Rev. Mr. Pond's ministry, by profession, two men and two women; during the vacancy following, two men, by letter; during Rev. Mr. Sparhawk's ministry, a hundred men and a hundred and forty-five women by profession, and nineteen men and thirty-four women by letter. This just completes the first half-century. In the second half, members have been received as follows: During the vacancy after Mr. Sparhawk's death, four men and four women by letter, and one woman by profession; and during Rev. Dr. Wellington's ministry, including the time since the settlement of a colleague, by profession, seventy-two men and a hundred and seventy-three women; by letter, eight men and twenty women.

The whole number received to this church in Mr. Sparhawk's ministry, by profession, was two hundred and forty-five. The number so received in Dr. Wellington's ministry, up to the close of the century, is also just two hundred and forty-five.

The whole number of members who have been dismissed and recommended during the century, or who have withdrawn for the purpose of joining other churches or of forming new ones, is a hundred and ninety-six, — eighty-two men and a hundred and fourteen women. Of these, five were dismissed to form the First Church in Hubbardston, which was organized in 1770; twenty-five, to form the church in Phillipston in 1785, or to join it soon after; three, to form the First Church in Gardner, at its organization in 1786; twenty, in all, to join the Baptist connection, — the church of that persuasion in this town being formed in 1782; twenty-eight, at various times, to become members of the Trinitarian church in this town, formed in 1832. Of the eighty-one foregoing, thirty-three were men; forty-eight, women. Three or four others, originally received as members here, now commune elsewhere, and not with us; having made no request for dismission. There have been dismissed and recommended to other churches during the century, in consequence of their removal to various places, a hundred and fifteen members, — forty-nine men and sixty-six women. A considerable number also have moved from the town, but without letters of dismission. One member only has been excluded.

The practice of "owning the covenant" for the purpose of having baptism for children, according to a pretty general custom of the times, was considerably practised in Mr. Sparhawk's ministry. It was adopted by the church, May 7, 1758, when they voted, "that parents and others, come to adult age, should receive the ordinance of baptism for themselves and theirs by virtue of owning the covenant, and thereto stand propounded two sabbaths." Under this vote, ninety-five persons have "owned the covenant" here, — forty-four men and fifty-one women; four of them in Rev. Mr. Pond's ministry, the rest in Mr. Sparhawk's, — almost all of them before 1780. A large number of these were afterward received to "full communion," and are included in the numbers already given. The vote just quoted has never been rescinded; the church expressly refusing to do so, July 30, 1807. But it has long been obsolete. In fact, no person has "owned the covenant" in that sense, in this church, since 1791.

During the century, there have been sixteen hundred and forty-one baptisms in this church. Twenty-three were in Rev. Mr. Pond's ministry, — all children. In Rev. Mr. Sparhawk's ministry, there were eleven hundred and sixteen, only ten of them adults; in Rev. Dr. Wellington's, the number is five hundred and two, of whom fifty-six were adults. In the two intervals, when there was a vacancy in the pastoral office, no baptisms are recorded.

The varying numbers of children baptized at different periods may serve to indicate the different states of public sentiment on the subject. Thus we find that the average of baptisms of children here, in the *first* half-century of the church, was twenty-two per annum; in the *second* half-century, the average number has been ten per annum. In the first seven years of Mr. Sparhawk's ministry, the population being at first but small, the number was a hundred and fifty-eight; but in the next fourteen years of his ministry, from 1768 to 1782, there were five hundred and sixty children baptized, — an average of just forty a year. Yet, in his *last* fourteen years, there were only a hundred and sixty-two, — an average of about twelve a year; and, of the children baptized in Dr. Wellington's ministry, more than four-fifths were in the first twenty-five years. This striking change, which has thus been progressing for upwards of sixty years, was of course promoted, in some part, by the formation of the Baptist society, and the influence of their views. But it is evident that the extent of the change has been far greater than can be ascribed to that source alone. This is not the occasion to offer any extended remark upon the subject; but I cannot refrain from suggesting, that the principal cause is to be found in the unscriptural and untenable views of the rite which were prevalent in the last century. There can be no doubt that infant baptism was then often regarded as, *in itself*, an *efficacious sacrament.* In the Roman-Catholic church, baptism, whether of infants or of others, had been regarded as a saving ordinance. The spiritual condition of a baptized child, whether living or dying, is deemed by the Roman Catholics wholly different from that of the unbaptized. After the Protestant Reformation, this rite, being still retained as a sacrament, continued to carry with it associations more or less similar. The Articles and Catechism of the Established Church of England, as well as the writings of many of her divines, strongly indicated the theory of baptismal regeneration of infants. In the theology of the Puritans, too, there was maintained to be an essential difference, as to their relations to the divine promises, between baptized and unbaptized children. These views, not derived, as we think, from Scripture, but inherited from the church of Rome, pervaded, to a great extent, the whole body of the people in New England, though with more or less vagueness of impression as to their doctrinal basis. They thought, that, in the act of baptism, the spiritual condition of the infant was then and there materially changed. I know of no evidence that Rev. Mr. Sparhawk himself held any such doctrine, and have reason to think he did not. But it is unquestionable, that ideas of the sort largely influenced the people throughout the country. This explains the fact, that so many infants, seventy-five and a hundred years ago, were baptized as soon as practicable after birth, very often during the first week of their lives. But such convictions gradually became weakened, or faded away. A corresponding alteration of the practice took place. The result has been, that now the number of baptisms of infants is everywhere small, compared with what it once was. It has served as an instructive lesson against permitting a religious usage to rest upon irrational grounds. But there *are* other grounds, of great significance, why parents should dedicate their offspring to God, in infancy, by this religious rite. Those grounds look to the usage, not as the observance of a *ritual law*, nor as undistinguished from the *personal* consecration and profession of faith which the adult believer makes of himself by receiving baptism, but rather as an impressive consecration and symbolic rite in which the parents are primarily concerned, and the child through them. When parents, believing in the gospel, thus testify their desire and intent that the child shall grow up under Christian nurture, and be regarded, from the first dawning of its intelligence, as dedicated to its heavenly Father, its Saviour, and the influences of the Divine Spirit bestowed from the Father through the Son, then the spiritual beauty and improvement of this rite is felt with power. May we not believe, that in coming times, on a more just and scriptural and practical foundation than was the usage of the past, such consecrations will become general in every Christian community?

The number of deaths in this town, or funerals attended, in the first half-century, was not recorded in the church-books; nor are there means for determining how many marriages were then solemnized.

I proceed to complete the statistics of the century, by giving the number of councils participated in for the settlement of ministers; and the elections of deacons. The number of ordaining or installing councils which this church has attended — one or more delegates being always appointed beside the pastor — is fifty-seven. Of these, twelve were in the first half-century, and forty-five in the second.

It has been the usual practice in this church to have three deacons. Five different persons were chosen and accepted during the first half-century, and five others during the second half. The first choice was made in March, 1763, of CHARLES BAKER, who lived on the Phillipston territory. He did not accept till the following year, upon a renewed election. He continued in office till the formation of the church in Gerry, in 1785. In 1767, two others were appointed, — Jonas Wilder, who had been chosen in December, 1763, and then declined, but now accepted; and Phineas Byam, who at first delayed his acceptance, but is called deacon in the records a few months after: he officiated for forty years. In 1780, Paul Kendall was elected deacon: he served about forty-five years. In 1789, Deacon Jonas Wilder having previously removed to Lancaster, N.H.; and Deacon Charles Baker been dismissed, to form, with others, the church in Gerry, — Josiah Wilder was appointed deacon, Timothy Parker having declined. He continued upwards of a quarter of a century. In 1807, on the death of Deacon Byam, Jonathan Cutting, sen., was elected: he resigned in 1830, at the age of upwards of eighty years. Upon the death of Deacon Josiah Wilder in 1818, Thomas Fisher was chosen. He died about four years afterward, and Deacon Ezekiel Partridge was appointed in his place. In 1825, Deacon Paul Kendall having resigned on account of his advanced age, the church chose his son Paul Kendall for successor: but he declined, as did also John Bigelow; and Deacon Jeremiah Lord was chosen. The vacancy caused by Deacon Cutting's resignation was filled, in 1830, by the election of Deacon Leonard Stone.

Such is the survey of our past history. It impresses us with a sense of gratitude to that Providence which watched over the feeble settlement, and has brought it to the days of its strength, and established its institutions. It impresses us also with a sense of reverence and honor for those true-hearted men who laid the foundations of what we so highly prize.

And now we have arrived at the threshold of the second century of our religious organizations here. We are looking forward to the future. What a flood of thoughts and profound emotions rush into the mind as we make the contemplation! *We* shall change, and pass away. A few years now suffice to make great alterations, by death and changes of residence, in any religious society. When even another half-century has gone, how few of all this congregation will be here! — how few of us then will be remaining on earth! And, as we think of this, let us to-day seriously put it to our consciences, how we are using our present privileges, and what we ought to ask God to enable us to do for the future. But, however it may be with any of *us*, these institutions of religion, as we trust, are to remain. The sacraments are still to be administered here, and the doors of the sanctuary opened for the public worship of God, in the name of his Son Jesus Christ, as it has been for a hundred years past. Here the Sunday school, with its gospel instructions and persuasions bearing upon the tender minds of the young, is to be perpetuated. The social influences of Christianity are to be cherished, and the beautiful neighborhood charities of our religion cultivated. And, as we look forward to the century now to come, what anticipations — joy and sorrow mingling, yet hope and encouragement predominating — fill the vista of the years! Great changes must be looked for in the future, as well as in the past. How extensive these changes may be, we know not. New forms and usages may displace the present, as ours, in some measure, have those of the past. More light may break forth from God's word. Christian philanthropy may find out new methods and new objects. Let us trust that this church will ever be candid toward all new claims, views, and obligations; that its members will ever seek to act up to the light God at any time giveth. But this we are sure of, that, amid whatever changes of forms and usages, *principles* do not change. There are central truths of religious faith and duty, not obscure, nor hard to receive, by which Christianity exercises all its practical power over men. These are likewise the everlasting principles, in harmony with which the Almighty's moral government over his children is perpetually administered. These, therefore, are the same yesterday, to-day, and for ever. The same God is for ever to be worshipped and obeyed; the same Saviour for ever trusted in as the Light of the world, as the divinely appointed Mediator for our salvation. And, in the coming century, on this basis we are to uphold and make effectual the institutions that have been transmitted to us. We are to build on the foundations of the past.

One hope and expectation cherished by the fathers is, indeed, to be disappointed. When they formed our present organization, they trusted and believed that their posterity here would be united together, on the broad basis of our simple Congregational platform and usages, into *one* church fellowship, — into one combined Christian co-operation. That anticipation is not fulfilled. But let us not lament over the divisions of the past. We may trust they were, at least in the main, conscientiously taken up. Those differences and separations were nothing peculiar to this town, but are similar to what God's providence has permitted to exist everywhere, perhaps to be overruled for greater results than we now comprehend. Consider how in the past, and now, doctrinal diversities have always accompanied freedom; and how many separations have arisen, in consequence, among those that alike acknowledge the authority of Jesus Christ, and receive the same written word. Surely it must be a disheartening contemplation to any one, whatever his own views may be, if he cannot think that all this is really of providential import. Sad and gloomy must be the anticipation to one who cannot think that — to be controlled, at length, by the power of the common faith in the one Lord and Master of us all — these diversities are working together as a part of that mighty combination of influences, guided by the Divine Spirit, which shall bring in the time when the nations of the world will become obedient unto our God and his Christ.

But let us judge as we may as to any doctrines or creeds in their abstract or practical import, the existing separations, while they continue, may be conducted honorably and amicably. We have agreed to differ. It remains for this church of Christ, on the foundation of its own conscientious convictions of truth and duty, to persevere, in the century to come, in fulfilling the trust we have received from the past. We are not chained down to any traditional, human articles of speculative doctrine. This church never adopted any sectarian name or pledges. It is not unity of doctrinal opinion that we need or require, but the loving surrender of the heart to Christ as the Lord of all; sincere repentance for sin; prayer and daily struggle for that "holiness without which no man shall see the Lord." In the oneness of this faith, in the bond of charity and peace, maintaining the same broad platform of fellowship as was here of old, we offer a cordial greeting to all, of every name, who take Christ for their Master and Saviour, and receive the Scriptures as containing the rule for their faith and practice. Accordingly, there are and always have been among us differences of views as to the meaning of passages of Scripture and as to doctrinal conclusions. Why should it not be so? Why should *not* neighbors and friends worship together and work together, and cherish a mutual fellowship, even if they *do* come to different conclusions on those points which have exercised the minds of thinking men for so many ages, and on which the wisest and best of mankind have differed? This is the position we take; and whether it is one right and safe, and for the good of the cause of religion, let experience and the judgment of posterity decide.

As we go forward in the coming century to the responsibilities that lie before us, let it be with gratitude and hope. We have the inheritance of our institutions from the past. We have its sacred memories to encourage us on. See to it, my friends, that you fulfil the duties which rest upon you to sustain these institutions. Cherish not only a care for the religious welfare of your own borders, but likewise an active and generous missionary spirit. Cultivate enlarged Christian sympathies with humanity everywhere. Cherish refined and ennobling social influences, attended by considerate and adequate charities. Take heed to all that belongs to the religious education of the young, not only in the Sunday school, but still more at home. Reverence all Christian rites. Encourage the regular attendance on public worship. Come into the house of God to offer personally the sacrifices of praise and prayer. Speak often one to another of these things. Bring hither hearts touched with a genuine contrition, and looking upward for the offered mercy. And, with the growth of your own faith, knowledge, piety, and charity, work onward in anticipation of the gradual diffusion, far and wide, of a free, pure, rational, practical Christianity. Let us try to do each our part "in this great work of ages." As we are blessed now by what the fathers handed down to us, at such cost and with such exertion on their part, so let *us* transmit what shall bless the generation to come. Meanwhile, it is for us to show the value of our faith by its fruits. The strength of that testimony to the century now before us will depend upon the tone and spirit of the Christian life that shall be nurtured here. It will be determined by the vigor and comprehensiveness of our benevolence; by the fidelity shown to our missionary duties; by the fervency and genuineness of our devotion, public and private; by the measure of our experience of the gospel's power to support the soul in temptation, in affliction, and in the hour of death.

God grant that here the persuasions of our religion may long continue to make their way to many hearts! Here may disciples of Christ long strengthen each other in every practical duty taught by our faith! Here may they unite, in hallowed sympathy, generation after generation, worshipping the common Father of all through the one only Saviour, and seeking the life-giving influences of the Holy Spirit and Comforter sent down from heaven!

APPENDIX.

Note A. — Page 4.

GRANT OF THE TOWNSHIP.

The lands here were regarded as the property of the Province of Massachusetts. The Legislature, in the last century, granted public lands more with reference to the policy of opening new settlements than with a view to making them a source of profit to the treasury. In 1728, application was made to the General Court for grants of wild lands in compensation for military services in the Narraganset-Indian War. The merciless destruction of those Indians and their habitations took place in 1675; but certain promises made to the soldiers to give them gratuities in land had never been fulfilled. Those claims, though fifty years old, were brought forward by the soldiers who survived and by the heirs of others, and were recognized by the General Court, June 15, 1728. It granted two townships, each of six miles square, and ordered notices to be posted up in every town in the Province, for soldiers and their representatives to present evidence of their claims. A convention of those who brought forward their claims was ordered to be held in the summer of 1730. They were ordered to meet, not in Boston, but in Cambridge, "by reason of the small-pox being then in Boston." At that meeting, the number of those entitled was found to be much larger than had been expected; and Thomas Tileston, Esq., and others, were made a committee to ask the General Court for more townships. They were directed by the General Court to meet again, in Boston, in the autumn, "as the distemper is now out of Boston." The petition for more land was acted upon favorably by the House of Representatives, Dec. 30, 1730; and it was determined, June 1, 1731, that every one hundred and twenty grantees should have six miles square of land. A list of those entitled to receive land was presented in the House of Representatives, and accepted, Jan. 17, 1731 (old style). The concurrence of the Executive Council and of the Governor was still necessary to give validity to the grant; there being no Senate during the Provincial government. On the next day, Jan. 18, the House of Representatives, anxious for the passage of the grant, sent a special message to the Council Board, urging the justice of the measure, and setting forth earnestly and eloquently the valor and merit of the soldiers engaged in the Narraganset expedition. The fact of the promises concerning land having been made to them was stated in this message in the following words: "A proclamation was made to the army, in the name of the government, when they were mustered on Dedham Plain, where they began their march, that if they played the man, took the fort, and drove the enemy out of the Narraganset country (which was their great seat), they should have a gratuity in land, beside their wages." In June, 1732, further claims of soldiers were allowed, under the authority of a committee; and a township was drawn by each one hundred and twenty. The township drawn at that time by our proprietors seems to have been within the territory of New Hampshire, "west of Ponocook and Suncook." The Narraganset township No. 3 was the present town of Mount Vernon, N.H.; and No. 5 was the present town of Bedford, N.H. But, in 1745, the courts decided that under the grant by King James I. to Capt. John Mason, in 1621, his great-grandson, John Tufton Mason, was entitled to an immense territory in New Hampshire, including the Narraganset townships above named. The titles to those lands, resting upon the grant from the General Court of Massachusetts, of course failed. The owners of the Mason title, however, were disposed to make liberal terms with actual settlers. In October, 1733, our proprietors, not liking the tract first assigned, voted to lay out a township here, "on the back of Rutland," — the boundaries of Rutland at that time comprehending Barre, which was called "Rutland District," — to be in place of the one they drew the year before at Boston; and, in February following, the location and survey were accepted and confirmed, agreeably to the following extract from the records of the General Court. The date is old style, and corresponds to Feb. 23, 1734: —

TUESDAY, Feb. 12, 1733.

A plat of a township for the Narraganset soldiers, bounded south-westerly on the township granted to Capt. Lovel's soldiers; * south-easterly mostly on Rutland,† and partly on the Narraganset township No. 2 by Wachusett; ‡ north-easterly partly on said township, and partly on unappropriated land, and partly on the new township laid out on Miller's River; § beginning at Rutland northerly corner, and running north thirty-nine degrees west by the needle, three hundred and ten perch, to a hemlock; from thence, west eighteen degrees north, three hundred and forty perch, to a white pine; from thence, north thirty-four degrees west, one thousand two hundred and eighty perch (to the said province town); from thence, south, three hundred perch, to a white pine; from thence, eight hundred and sixty perch, to a beach-tree, the north-easterly corner of the said town granted to Capt. Lovel's soldiers; from thence, south thirty-four degrees east, one thousand eight hundred and twenty-four perch, to a heap of stones in Rutland line; from thence, east thirty degrees north, to the place where it began: — being the contents of six miles square, and an allowance of three hundred acres for the Mine Farm (so called), and a hundred acres for a pond in said tract.

In the House of Representatives, read, and ordered that the plat be accepted, and that the lands set forth and described in the within plat of the Narraganset township No. 6 (exclusive of the Mine Farm, so called) be and hereby are confirmed to a hundred and twenty of the original grantees, their heirs and assigns, — viz., that

---

* Petersham. † The part which is now Barre. ‡ Westminster. § Athol.

society of them of which Mr. Samuel Chandler and others were appointed a committee for regulating the said township No. 6 (so called), at a general meeting of the grantees the 6th of June, as by their votes and orders may appear, — provided the plat contains no more than the quantity of land within mentioned, and does not interfere with any former grants.

In Council, read, and concurred.

Consented to, J. BELCHER [*Governor*].

NOTE B. — PAGE 8.

FORTY-ACRE HOUSE-LOTS.

These lots were designed for earliest cultivation. The committee appointed by the proprietors to lay out the lots consisted of Samuel Chandler, James Jones, Joshua Richardson, John Longley, and Joseph Fassett. Mr. Chandler and his son were paid for twenty-three days' time in lotting out the town. Jonas Houghton, and Messrs. Hosmer, Jones, and Farrar, were paid, June 25, 1735, for their services as surveyors. There must have been considerable inconvenience and want of economy in the mode adopted of laying out all the forty-acre lots before it had been fully decided where the roads of the township should be located; though, in a portion of the surveyed lots, mention is made of reservations for roads through them. It was, moreover, voted, in January following, that any proprietors that should "be uneasy with the lots they had drawn have liberty to drop them, and lay out forty-five acres of any of the upland not lotted out, doing it at their own cost, within two years [and making their lots], in a regular form." May 8, 1751, similar leave was granted, provided it should be done within six weeks, and the quantity taken not more than forty acres. It was a condition of the grant by the Legislature, that sixty families should be settled on as many lots within seven years. In 1737, it was voted by the proprietors, that the owners of sixty of the lots, designated by drawing numbers, should pay into the treasury the sum of twelve pounds each, old tenor, and that the other sixty lots should be settled within three years, and that each proprietor who settled his lot should receive eight pounds from the treasury out of the money paid by the "non-settlers." But it was not found practicable to effect settlements so early. The General Court allowed some delay; and it was voted, Sept. 16, 1742, that any, who, within two years from that time, would settle their lots according to the required terms, should be entitled to the eight pounds. But settlers did not come in; and the proprietors voted, in 1743, to give twelve pounds, old-tenor currency, additional to the former bounty, to each of the first ten or any smaller number of families, who, before Sept. 1, 1744, would "build a good dwelling-house, and inhabit the same, agreeably to the act of the Great and General Court, and be an inhabitant in said township at that time." But the war between France and England which immediately came on, and in which many Indian tribes were engaged as allies of the French, wholly suspended, for several years, all plans of building, or cultivating land, within the township. The proprietors held no meeting for the transaction of business between March, 1744, and October, 1749; peace having been declared previous to the last-named date.

Note C. — Page 10.

MINE HILL.

The idea of the existence of mines in this township seems to have rested upon the peculiarities of Mine Hill, near the Hubbardston line. The hill and its neighborhood abound in sulphuret of iron. Whitney's History of Worcester

County, published in 1793, states that this hill was granted to Capt. Andrew Robinson, of Gloucester, some time before the original grant of the township. I have made search, in the records at the State House,* to find the time and conditions of this grant to Capt. Robinson, but without success. Some record, however, may exist.

It will be noticed, that, in the grant by the General Court of the title to this township, mention is made of allowing three hundred acres extra, in the dimensions of the surveyed plot, in consideration of reserving the Mine Farm from the grant. That tract was finally sold by vote of the proprietors in 1787. The land being contained within their boundaries, it might have been considered that the ancient grant prior to theirs had lapsed in their favor. It would seem, however, that the legal title must have been either in the representatives of Capt. Robinson, or in the Commonwealth. According to Whitney's History, a company of gentlemen from Boston and elsewhere undertook, previous to the first settling of the town, to carry on mining on that hill. He says, "They dug several rods into the hill in quest of a silver mine; but whether it answered their expectations or not, was not divulged." We may safely presume it *did not;* though Mr. Whitney seems to suppose the work would have been carried further, had it not been for the breaking out of the French and Indian War, and that rich mines might, not improbably, really exist there. The knowledge of the existence of such an excavation was for a long time lost. The cave was discovered in 1824. It extends fifty-seven feet and a half, dug into the solid rock.

Note D. — Page 27.

The following extract from Rev. Mr. Buckminster's Sermon at the ordination of Mr. Sparhawk (pp. 11, 12) may serve as a specimen, and to justify the commendation given in the discourse. They are noble sentiments, and as fitting now as they were a century ago:—

Ministers should, by rights, have no little insight into the original languages (those in which the Scriptures were written), that they may drink at the fountain where the waters are purest, no foot having defiled them; that they may see with their own eyes, and not take every thing upon trust from others, be led away by the error of the wicked, and stand exposed to crafty men who lie in wait to deceive; but that they may be capable, if need be, to contend earnestly for the faith, and to confute gainsayers. They should be, in some measure, acquainted with the liberal arts and sciences, which serve to open and enlarge the mind, and are all handmaids to divinity. But religion itself should be their principal study. The religion of the Bible should be that, which, above all things, they are not ignorant of. They should be, Apollos-like, men mighty in the Scriptures, and accordingly, more than others, addict themselves to the means and methods of information; get wisdom, and, with all their gettings, get understanding. They should give attendance to reading, no less than exhortation and doctrine (the one will render them capable of the other); neglect not the gift that is in them, which was given by prophecy, whether with or without the laying on the hands of the presbytery; meditate upon these things, give themselves wholly to them, that their profiting may appear unto all, or, in all things. Truth should be the object of their pursuit,—sacred truth. What is truth? should be the question they would ever decide. They should therefore lay aside, as much as may be, prepossession and prejudice; lay their minds open to conviction; not be carried away with an affectation of novelty and singularity, any more than shackled with authority and venerable antiquity. They should dare to embrace and adhere to unpopular truth, as well as to renounce popular error.

Note E.—Page 28.

CHANGE OF PRICES.

In comparing the standard of prices at the present time with the standard as it was eighty or a hundred years ago, there are many particulars to be considered, some of which have varied in a very different ratio from others.

But the following items, among others, will tend to justify the statement in the Discourse respecting the comparative value of money in 1761 and now. In the interval between Mr. Pond's dismission and Mr. Sparhawk's ordination, — i.e., from 1759 to 1761, — the price for boarding the minister *and his horse* was eight shillings a week; *now* it would be considerably more than three times as much. In 1755, the common price of beef was between two and three cents a pound; poultry, the same; rye was about two shillings and eightpence a bushel; butter, nine cents a pound, or less; labor, in the summer season, at farm-work, two shillings a day. In 1762, and for some years afterwards, the price for a man and a yoke of oxen in June, at highway-work, was seventy-five cents a day, without board. In 1755, the price for a man and a yoke of oxen was but four shillings a day: horses were kept for nine cents a day. Horse-hire, at various times between 1760 and 1795, was no more than from two to three cents a mile. School-teachers, for the first fifteen years after the incorporation of the town, had less than one-quarter of what is now usual. The board of the male teachers was then seventy-eight cents a week; of females, forty-six cents. The gradual increase of teachers' wages is an important index of the advancing standard of prices as to the expenses of professional men. It appears, that, in this town, the wages of teachers rather more than doubled in the forty years between 1765 and 1805; and, since 1805, the compensation of teachers has fully doubled *again*, so as to be upwards of four times as much at the present time as it was in 1770. It may be noted, as a corresponding circumstance, that, in the forty years between 1767 and 1807, the price of a day's work for a man and a pair of oxen a little more than doubled, and that the price *now* is also about double what it was in 1807; so that, in the ninety years, the price for such work has increased about fourfold. As late as 1788 and 1791, the repairs on the meeting-house cost only four shillings a day for carpenter-work (boarding themselves); and fifty cents a day for painters, with five shillings a week for their board. In 1799, mason-work was one dollar a day, without board.

The rise that has taken place in the standard of prices was by no means dependent merely on the town's being newly settled: it is a part of a general and inevitable movement, in which the whole civilized world shares. The advance has been somewhat more rapid in this country than in Europe. For example, Macaulay estimates, that, in a period of a hundred and fifty years, the compensation of mercantile clerks in England has increased threefold; and the wages of agricultural laborers and of mechanics, between two and three fold. This advance in the standard of prices is something which must inevitably go on, both in this country and in Europe, in the century to come. Nor is it to be lamented. It is a change, which, in the long run, operates in favor of the prosperity and thrift of the laboring portion of the community, as compared with capitalists; and every thing which increases the comparative comfort of the families of laboring men, and their means of education, has a direct tendency to promote good morals, and is for the advantage of society in all respects.

Note F. — Pages 32, 37.

RESULT OF COUNCIL.

The following is a copy of the result of the Ecclesiastical Council called by Mr. Sparhawk and the church: —

Templeton, June 7, 1780.

At an Ecclesiastical Council convened in the First Precinct in Templeton, agreeably to letters-missive from the church in said precinct: Present the following pastors and messengers of the churches; viz.: —

Pastors.	*Messengers or Delegates.*
Rev. Daniel Emerson .	Mr. Moses Thurston.
Rev. Zabdiel Adams .	Lieut. Caleb Taylor.
Rev. Josiah Dana . .	John Mason, Esq., and Capt. Ezra Jones.
Rev. Joseph Brown .	Dea. Moses Hale and Dr. Israel Whiton.
Rev. Joseph Lyman .	Capt. Elisha Allis.

The Rev. Mr. Emerson was chosen Moderator; and the Rev. Joseph Brown, Scribe. The Council was opened by prayer to God for light and influence; then proceeded to enter upon the business for which we are called; and, the better to accomplish the good design of their appointment, chose a Committee of Council to treat with the dissenting brethren of the church, and sundry other inhabitants of the precinct who were dissatisfied with the calling of said Council. The Committee attended the business of their appointment, and made report, that they were unable to persuade the persons to whom they were sent to enter upon a friendly conference with the Council. Being unsuccessful in this expedient, the Council proceeded to a public hearing in the meeting-house, where we opened with prayer by the Moderator; then heard the various votes and papers which the pastor and church had to lay before us. Without entering into a minute description of these votes and papers, we shall give our opinion upon the matters referred to for our consideration in the rule of submission. We first took up the third article of said rule, in which our judgment is desired upon sundry votes and proceedings of the church, &c. We are persuaded that the determination of this church, in refusing communion with Mr. Walley's church in Bolton, was agreeable to gospel order, and was therefore no just ground of uneasiness and dissatisfaction to the dissenting brethren; and that Rev. Mr. Sparhawk's conduct in entering his dissent against certain votes of the church, and, in particular, his non-concurring the vote of communion with Mr. Walley's church, formerly passed, and which he could not in conscience carry into execution, being a matter of privilege in the pastor, was no just foundation of discontentment in the minds of the brethren. Also that the pastor's refusal to call a church-meeting, in conformity to the request of Jonas Wilder and others, dated April 5, 1777, should not be viewed as just matter of uneasiness by the signers of that application, for the reasons given by the Rev. Mr. Sparhawk.

In respect of the church's proceedings with Mr. Abijah Kendall, we are of opinion that they had just right to suspend him from acting with them, for the reasons specified in their votes.

We are sorry to find that imputations have been cast upon the pastor, of unfriendliness to the rights and privileges of his country. We think that there is sufficient evidence of his attachment to the civil interests of these States, and that he merits the confidence of his people, as a friend to the laws and liberties of this Commonwealth.

As our sentiments are requested respecting the precinct-meeting held May 22, 1780, we cannot, in fidelity, omit to suggest, that matters of ecclesiastical controversy are to be brought before ecclesiastical bodies only; and that any attempts to bring the religious conduct of Christians, and the powers and privileges of the church, before a civil jurisdiction, are highly dangerous, and unwarrantable; and therefore the pastor and church, in refusing to attend that precinct-meeting, considered as held for the abovesaid purposes, conducted in a manner justifiable and commendable; and that the conduct of those two church-members who endeavored to bring him upon trial before that meeting was highly offensive in the sight of God.

In reference to the pastor's desire of advice under his difficulties respecting his support, and as to his dismission from his ministerial office, we find, from the word of God, that ministers have a clear and scriptural right to a decent and honorable support from the people whom they serve. Mr. Sparhawk, we think, has not been thus supported for several years; but, notwithstanding the troubles and embarrassments he has labored under, we cannot but recommend to him further trial and patience, to see if the people will not comply with their interest and duty in affording him a competent maintenance. But, should he be unable to obtain a redress of his sufferings, we cannot advise him to continue much longer in such a state of oppression; but, according to the gospel, to shake off the dust of his feet as a testimony against those who refuse to fulfil the solemn obligations they are under by their own covenant, as well as by the word of God. And, should he be under the necessity of seeking a dismission, we advise him, after such forbearance as his Christian prudence and discretion shall dictate, to call in, with the consent of the church, a council of three sister churches to assist and advise in the separation.

As to the conduct of the dissenting brethren in disagreeing with the church in their votes, we advise the church not to entertain any uneasiness with their brethren for a difference of sentiment in the matters which have been controverted for several years among them.

Thus, brethren, we have attended to the matters which you have thought fit to lay before us. We are anxiously distressed to find that such wide breaches have been made upon you; that the Spirit of holiness and peace has so far withdrawn his blessed influences from you, and left you to such unhappy jealousies and animosities. We humbly supplicate the Father of all mercies to pour out his blessed influences into your hearts, and to point out to you the path of duty and peace. We wish the pastor, while he goes before you, to show himself a pattern of gentleness and condescension; conforming himself in all matters (as far as will comport with a good conscience towards God) to the views and desires of his beloved flock; using his authority as pastor with tenderness, not to the distraction, but for the edification, of the body of Christ in this place.

The people we would exhort to receive their pastor in love; to submit themselves to him in the Lord, and to account him worthy of double honor; to make his life comfortable, by affording a suitable support; and give none occasion of uneasiness to him who naturally cares for their good, and watches for their souls as one who must give an account.

We deplore what we forbode as the unhappy consequences of a separation and dissolution of the pastoral relation of this wise and good shepherd to this flock of our Lord's fold, which he has purchased with his own blood. May our ears soon be saluted with the happy tidings that your contentions are healed; that the God of truth and love hath returned to dwell among you; that his Spirit, in abundant measure, hath been showered down upon the pastor and people of this precinct; and that the hearts of all are turned to each other as the heart of one man! That such may be the blessed consequence of our painful and anxious labors, is our devout supplication to Almighty God for you; unto whom, and to the word of his grace, which is able to build you up, and to give you an inheritance among all them which are sanctified, we now commend you, through Jesus Christ our Lord. Amen.

By order and in the name of the Council,

DANIEL EMERSON, *Moderator.*

NOTE G. — PAGE 56.

RELIGIOUS SOCIETIES.

The following is an account of all the other Societies, beside the First Parish, which have maintained public worship in this town, arranged in order of the dates of their formation: —

The Baptist Church in this town was organized Aug. 22, 1782, at which time twenty-one members entered into covenant. It has had ten settled pastors. Rev. John Sellon, of English birth, was the first, and ordained Nov. 19, 1783.

He continued but a year and a half. Rev. Joel Butler became pastor in 1787, and remained four years. For eight or nine years after his dismission, the pulpit was supplied only upon temporary engagements, but with no settled minister; yet, during six years of this time, sixty-seven members were received to the church by baptism. Rev. Elisha Andrews became its pastor in the year 1800; was dismissed March 17, 1813, but re-installed in the spring of 1827, and finally dismissed in 1832,—making eighteen years, in all, of his ministry. During the interval of Mr. Andrews's absence, there were two pastors settled; but they continued not more than a year or two each: viz., Rev. George Phippen, settled March, 1821; and Rev. J. Parsons, settled December, 1824. The same year of Rev. Mr. Andrews's final dismission, Rev. Winthrop Morse was installed, September, 1832; and he was pastor about two years. Rev. Isaiah C. Carpenter was ordained Feb. 8, 1837, and resigned in 1843. Rev. John Woodbury was settled January, 1844; Rev. Sandford Leach, April, 1848; and Rev. A. V. Dimock, who is the pastor at the present time, was settled April 1, 1851. The first meeting-house of the Baptist Society was erected, in 1798 and 1799, at what is called the Baptist Common. The dedication-sermon was preached by the Rev. Dr. Baldwin, of Boston, in the autumn of 1799. In 1840 the meeting-house was removed to its present location in Baldwinville Village, and was opened and re-dedicated Feb. 3, 1841.

The Trinitarian Congregational Church in Templeton was organized April 11, 1832, and was constituted with twenty-four members. Since its organization, two hundred and forty-seven members have been added, including those by letter as well as by profession. A hundred and fifty-two have been dismissed, removed, or died. The meeting-house was built in 1833. The church has had two pastors. Rev. Lemuel P. Bates was installed Jan. 16, 1833, and was dismissed April 19, 1837. Rev. Lewis Sabin was installed Sept. 21, 1837, and is the pastor at the present time.

A Universalist Society was organized in 1842, and held its meetings in the old Town House. Not long after, Rev. Gerard Bushnell, who had been the preacher almost from the first, became stated pastor of the society, though without a formal installation; and he supplied, for the most part, while the meetings continued. No meeting-house was ever erected; but the society has held its worship in the present Town Hall, meeting on alternate Sundays, or at other stated intervals. At present, the society has no preaching.

In 1843, Rev. Willard Smith was appointed by the Conference of the Methodist Episcopal Church to supply as preacher in Templeton, in connection with South Royalston. A "class," included in the charge of preachers at Hubbardston, had been maintained for about three years previously. A church was formed, of twenty-four members, in 1843. The whole number of its members, beside those received only on probation, has been sixty-eight. A meeting-house, since disposed of, was erected in 1844. Rev. Mr. Smith was succeeded by Rev. John T. Pettee, who was appointed for Templeton, August, 1844. Rev. Simon Putnam was the minister from 1845 to 1847. In June, 1847, Rev. T. G. Brown was appointed; one or two other societies being also connected with Templeton under his charge. Preaching in the meeting-house of the society was discontinued from 1848. Meetings have been held a part of the time, since, in the East Village; but no preacher has been appointed by the Conference to make stated supply, except Rev. J. L. Estey, in 1852, in connection with South Royalston.

Congregations for public worship, under the ministry of preachers of the Second-Advent persuasion, had been held for some time previous to 1851, chiefly in the East Village. March 8, of that year, the Advent Church was organized, having twenty-one members at the time, with the Rev. C. R. Griggs, pastor. He resides in another town, but continues to be the minister. The meetings for public worship have been held, for the most part, on alternate Sundays.

Public worship, according to the forms of the Roman-Catholic Church, has been conducted occasionally, within the last eight or ten years, but not at stated intervals, in private houses in the Factory Village in this town; chiefly by Rev. Mr. Gibson, a priest of that order, who was of English birth. In 1853, under his auspices, and by means of liberal contributions on the part of those attending upon his ministrations, an edifice, costing about $2,000, was erected for their use; and it was "consecrated" in 1854. It is called St. Martin's Chapel. Since that time, religious services have been conducted in it one Sunday in every four. Rev. Mr. Gibson officiated there about two years, residing in Fitchburg; but, having returned to his native country, Rev. Mr. Turpin, of Fitchburg, has since officiated.

NAMES OF PROPRIETORS OF THE TOWNSHIP IN 1735.

The following is a list of the proprietors who originally drew the forty-acre lots, or "house-lots" as they were called, in the first division of lands made at the proprietors' meeting at Concord, Jan. 24, 1735 (old style). It happened, at the time of drawing, that No. 107 was not used. Nos. 71, 72, being "mine-lots," — that is, falling on Mine Hill, — were reserved; and so duplicates were drawn for Nos. 94, 95, and 96, and these were distinguished as 94 east, 94 west, 95 east, &c.: —

No. of Lot.	
1.	Hezekiah Hapgood.
2.	Benjamin Hatterton.
3.	Jonathan Farnsworth.
4.	Thomas Baldwin.
5.	John Overing, Esq.
6.	Nathaniel Trask.
7.	Samuel Hartwell.
8.	Ephraim Brown.
9.	Simon Davis.
10.	William Wheeler.
11.	Daniel Gates.
12.	Benjamin Thompson.

No. of Lot.		No. of Lot.	
13.	Thomas Baldwin.	60.	Jonathan Bowers.
14.	Samuel Miles.	61.	Benjamin Smith.
15.	Simon Stone.	62.	Henry Baldwin.
16.	Timothy Townsend.	63.	Thomas Tarbell.
17.	Jonathan Whitcomb.	64.	Samuel Sargeant.
18.	George Farrar.	65.	Jacob Wright.
19.	Benjamin Temple.	66.	Henry Eames.
20.	John Priest.	67.	Col. Benjamin Prescott.
21.	Ephraim Twitchell.	68.	James Houghton.
22.	Robert Robbins.	69.	Ebenezer Wheeler.
23.	Nathan Brooks.	70.	Daniel Woodward.
24.	Samuel Shelden.	73.	John Longley.
25.	John Wheeler.	74.	Benjamin Shedd.
26.	John Wood.	75.	Thomas Amsden.
27.	Joseph Horsley.	76.	Simon Davis.
28.	Joshua Richardson.	77.	Nathaniel Kendall.
29.	William Shattuck.	78.	Robert Cummings.
30.	John Wyman.	79.	Thomas Ball.
31.	Edward Willson.	80.	John Bulkley.
32.	Joseph Wood.	81.	Jonathan Farr.
33.	Col. Benjamin Prescott.	82.	David Whitney.
34.	Zachariah Lawrence.	83.	David Stone.
35.	Zachariah Flagg.	84.	Moses Whitney.
36.	For support of schools.	85.	Jacob Wright.
37.	Col. Benjamin Prescott.	86.	Samuel Hunt.
38.	Samuel Stone.	87.	Thomas Amsden.
39.	Jonathan Buttrick.	88.	Zachariah Symmes.
40.	Samuel Warner.	89.	Jonathan Wyman.
41.	Daniel Gates.	90.	Caleb Sawyer.
42.	Eleazar Bateman.	91.	Josiah Hobbs.
43.	John Adams.	92.	For support of ministry.
44.	James Patterson.	93.	John Overing, Esq.
45.	Jacob Houghton.	94 E.	Joseph Wheat.
46.	For the first minister.	94 W.	Eleazar Flagg.
47.	Jonathan Simonds.	95 E.	John Muzzey.
48.	Moses Burdue.	95 W.	Ebenezer Parker.
49.	Samuel Chandler.	96 E.	Joseph Wheelock.
50.	John Eames.	96 W.	Samuel Willson.
51.	Thankful Reed.	97.	Edward Phelps.
52.	Samuel Chandler.	98.	Benjamin Whitney.
53.	Joseph Fassett.	99.	James Jones.
54.	Jonathan Lawrence.	100.	David Roberts.
55.	John Whitcomb, Esq.	101.	Col. Prescott.
56.	Timothy Spaulding.	102.	John Barrett.
57.	John Swan.	103.	John Cutter.
58.	Benjamin Gary.	104.	Elnathan Jones.
59.	John Cummings.	105.	Isaac Learnard.

No. of Lot.	
106.	John Needham.
108.	Thomas Hapgood.
109.	Thomas Hapgood.
110.	Henry Bartlett.
111.	Daniel Billings.
112.	Samuel Hincher.
113.	Edward Winn.
114.	Gershom Flagg.
115.	Ebenezer Fisk.
116.	James Simonds.
117.	Abraham Taylor.
118.	Daniel Adams.
119.	John Provender.
120.	David Wheeler.
121.	Benjamin Wyman.
122.	Daniel White.
123.	Elisha Tattingham.

Very few of these original owners actually settled here in person.

ORIGINAL DIVISION OF LANDS IN THE TOWNSHIP.

The first step towards dividing the territory among the proprietors was taken at a meeting held in Concord, Oct. 30, 1734, when it was—

Voted that the township be laid out in part as soon as may be. Voted that there be laid out a hundred and twenty-three forty-acre lots of the best of the upland. Chose a Committee of five to lay out the lots as above mentioned. Voted that the lots be made as equal as may be, and in as regular a form and as compact as the land will allow of. Voted that said Committee order *ways*, and where the meeting-house and the three public lots shall be, and to order land for a burying-place and for a training-place, and for other public use, according to their best discretion.

Agreeably to the foregoing vote, Samuel Chandler, of Concord, the proprietors' clerk, with others of the Committee, proceeded to lay out the hundred and twenty-three forty-acre lots, or "house-lots" as they were called,—one for each owner of the township, and the three public lots. They employed surveyors, and spent about thirty days in the work. They bought "a kittle" at the proprietors' expense. They paid Nathaniel Wilder and John Wilder for "bringing horses into the woods;" that is, into the township. They moreover purchased four bushels of oats, and spent six shillings and ninepence beside, "on the Publick accompt, when going into the woods."

At a meeting at Concord, Jan. 24, 1735 (old style), each proprietor's lot was "drawn out;" that is, determined by the number which fell to him in a chance drawing. Proprietors who did not like their lots were allowed to drop them, and take a similar quantity in the undivided land, provided they did so within certain times.

The settlement of the town having been delayed, as elsewhere stated, on account of Indian hostilities, no further division of land among the proprietors was attempted till May 9, 1750; when, at a meeting held in the township, "at the meeting-house place," it was voted to divide the meadow-land forthwith; and that "*four acres* in the middling sort of the meadow in said township be the standard (that is, four acres to be the quantity assigned to each proprietor); and that the Committee to be chosen shall have power to lay more or less as to quantity, making said lots equally good to the proposed standard, according to their best judgment." It was further voted, "that, in case the meadow-lands should not hold out so that each proprietor can have his proposed share therein, the said Committee shall have power to lay them out an equivalent, in swamp or upland, according to their best judgment, at the option of the person concerned; it being done in some regular form." John Whitcomb and Charles Baker were appointed surveyors. It was "voted that the Committee have four shillings a day, they supporting themselves; and that the surveyors have the same allowance, with their extraordinary charges allowed them." The meadow did not hold out to give each one four acres. At a meeting in Lancaster, at Mr. Samuel Locke's tavern, June 27, 1750, it was voted, that, in the drawing of the meadow, those who drew "blanks" should have *nine acres* each "in any of the undivided land, at the option of the person concerned," as a substitute for the four acres of meadow. At this meeting, the division was made by drawing lots; viz., eighty-five meadow-lots and thirty-eight blanks.

On the 11th September, 1751, it was voted "to come to a second division of upland; that *seventy acres* shall be the standard; and that the Committee shall have power to lay out the lots bigger or less, according to their goodness." These 123 seventy-acre lots having been surveyed accordingly, they were distributed by lot, May 13, 1752.

The next distribution was agreed upon in May, 1753,—*forty acres* to be the standard,—"and voted that every proprietor may 'pitch' to his own land; and that said Committee qualify said land over or under the standard, as it is for goodness or accommodation."—"Voted that those of the propriety that cannot 'pitch' to their own land have their land laid out and drawn for as formerly." This Committee were to have three shillings and sixpence per day, and the surveyors four shillings a day. A little more than half of these forty-acre lots, of the third division of upland, were "pitched;" that is, laid out by the recipients adjoining to their own previously distributed lots. The number of "pitched lots" was sixty-six: the other fifty-seven proprietors "drew" for locations.

No further distribution took place till twelve years later, and after the town had been incorporated; when, at a proprietors' meeting, Sept. 25, 1765, it was "voted to lay out a division in the common or undivided lands in said town, and that *twenty acres* be the standard for said division; and that the land be qualified by a Committee, and laid under or over the standard as to quantity, so as to make each lot as equal, as to goodness, as may be." Each proprietor was to have liberty "to pitch his lot:" "those that can, and are so disposed, to pitch to their own land; and those that cannot, to draw for their pitch." On the day of the meeting, fifteen persons, owning twenty-five and a half rights, pitched adjoining their own lands; and thirty-nine persons, owning forty-three rights, drew for their pitch.

Twelve years later, — viz., Oct. 29, 1777, — it was agreed that there should be a "fifth division" (that is, fifth division in addition to the division of the meadow), and that "the standard" of quantity to each one of the original hundred and twenty-three rights should be *six acres*, with similar regulations as to selection of locations as in the fourth division.

When lots had been laid out in these several distributions of land, the survey was usually laid before a meeting of the proprietors, and recorded by the proprietors' clerk. In those surveys and records, therefore, is to be found the description, courses, and bounds on which ultimately rested the titles, as regards individuals, to nearly all the land in town. It may therefore be useful here to mention, that, at the end of vol. ii. of the Proprietors' Records, there is a very valuable index to find the book and page where are recorded the lots belonging to each of the original rights or shares in the township, as assigned to the several proprietors in each of the six divisions.*

After the division of 1777, there still remained a quantity of land, in various strips and gores, of irregular shape, which belonged in common, or rather to the holders of the original rights as an incorporation. In 1786, May 3, at a meeting of the proprietors, a Committee having reported that the quantity of undivided land was about nine hundred acres, "lying in such forms and figures, and the land so unfit for improvement, and as it must cost a considerable sum to divide the same, and as the proprietors are now considerably in debt," "it is expedient to sell the same at public vendue, and, after paying the debts, divide the proceeds among the proprietors according to their interest," — this proposition was adopted; any proprietor, who should prefer it, being permitted to lay out his proportion in the undivided lands, before sale, under the direction of a Committee, by paying his part of the debts. June 6, 1787, it was agreed that the

---

* Six divisions; that is, inclusive of the meadows.

hill "called the Mine Hill" should be sold "at public vendue for the most it will fetch." After paying the debts, there was found a balance of eleven shillings and sixpence belonging to each original right, which the treasurer was directed to pay to the respective owners thereof.

It will be seen that each of the hundred and twenty-three original rights was entitled, in these divisions, to a quantity of land, intended to be equal, upon the average, to a hundred and eighty acres. Probably the quantity for each right, on the average, somewhat exceeded in the survey this standard; and I believe it is usually found, in modern surveys of farms in this town, that the old surveys included somewhat larger tracts than their specified quantities. Multiplying 180 acres by 123, the product is 22,140 acres. To this is to be added the hundred and ninety acres excess of upland allowed to those who had no meadow; the nine hundred acres sold at the closing up in 1787, with the land at first reserved on Mine Hill; also the land occupied by all the roads then laid out in the township, and by the Common, the burying-grounds, &c. The probability, therefore, seems to be, that the township, as originally laid out, included at least 25,000 acres. "Six miles square, with allowance of three hundred acres for the Mine Farm, and a hundred acres for a pond in said tract" (in Phillipston), which was the quantity specified by the General Court, would have been 23,440 acres. It is plain, therefore, that there was considerable excess in the original dimensions of the township over what the General Court intended.

VALUE OF LAND IN THE EARLY TIMES.

Before any settlements had been made here, the proprietors, wishing to secure a mill-privilege situated on Mr. Josiah Hobbs's forty-acre lot (of the first division), purchased, Aug. 24, 1743, his whole original right for £26. 10s.

on twelve months credit,—equal to £25 in money down. This was lot No. 91: it was situated in the present East Village. The money was payable, not in bills of old-tenor currency, but in Province bills "of the last emission," which, in 1743, were as good as silver, or nearly so. As there were a hundred and twenty private original rights in addition to the three public ones in the township, including the Phillipston portion, this would make the whole township, if sold at the same rate, worth just *ten thousand dollars*; and, as there was not very far from twenty-five thousand acres in the township, that would be at the rate of about *forty cents an acre* for the land, upon an average, making no allowance for any extra value in Mr. Hobbs's lot on account of the mill-privilege. The proprietors deeded this lot—No. 91—nine years afterwards, to Reuben and Oliver Richardson, for twenty-six pounds. As soon as the township became partially settled, and non-resident owners had advanced money, by way of taxes on their lots, for roads, &c., of course the lots became more valuable. Most of the original proprietors transferred their rights before any settlements took place. Little information can now be procured as to the prices. By examination at the Registry of Deeds at Worcester, however, it appears that one whole right was sold in 1744, and several others—original rights—were sold between 1753 and 1761 by committees of the proprietors for non-payment of taxes. Quite a number of other parcels of land—parts of lots—were deeded from one individual to another during the same period. I give the result of this examination, as to prices, in a number of cases. All the whole original lots sold for taxes, it will be observed, went at lower prices than No. 91 above mentioned.

1744, Nov. 26. Whole lot No. 7 sold for taxes, deeded to John Brooks for £16. 18s. 8d., lawful money.
1753, Nov. 7. Lot No. 65 deeded to Ebenezer Roby for £18. 16s.
1753, Nov. 7. Lot No. 61 to David Wilder for £15. 14s. 8d.
1754, Jan. 2. Lot No. 2 to Thomas Stoddard for £24. 13s. 4d.
1754, Dec. 31. Lot No. 96 to Nathaniel Longley for £14.

The average price of these five original rights would be equal to about thirty cents an acre.

The proprietors also sold for taxes several parcels of land, as follows: —

1756, July 8.	To Samuel Sawyer, $9\frac{1}{4}$ acres, at 2s. 8d. per acre.
1757, Jan. 10.	To Phineas Byam, 4 acres and 70 rods, at 4s. per acre.
1757, Jan. 4.	To Joseph Horsley, $10\frac{1}{8}$ acres, at 3s. 4d. per acre.
1758, Sept. 22.	To James Kendall, $11\frac{1}{2}$ acres of land, set off in the third division of lands to John Bulkley's original right, at 1s. $4\frac{3}{4}$d. per acre.
1759, Feb. 8.	To James Pierce, 4 acres, set off in second division of lands, at 3s. 6d. per acre.
1757, Jan. 20.	To Rev. Daniel Pond, $22\frac{1}{2}$ acres, at $9\frac{1}{2}$d. per acre.
1760, Mar. 20.	Zachariah Emory deeded to William Fletcher 4 acres of meadow, which was the original allotment of John Barrett, for £4. 16s., — equal to $4 an acre.
1752, Nov. 8.	Samuel Miles deeded to Reuben Miles 42 acres and 4 rods, "with allowance for roads," — situated "on the north side of Ladder Hill," — for £26. 13s. 4d. (This was equal to about two dollars and ten cents an acre. But it was laid out as an equivalent for one of the forty-acre lots of the *first division*, and therefore considered much better than the *average* of the land of the whole township.)

SAW-MILL AND GRIST-MILL.

At the proprietors' meeting at Concord, Jan. 24, 1735, a Committee was authorized "to agree with any person or persons that will erect a mill or mills in said township." This Committee, soon after, contracted with Mr. Samuel Sheldon, of Billerica, to build a saw-mill and a grist-mill. Mr. Sheldon gave bonds to erect the mills, of which he was to be the owner; and he was to receive a grant of land for establishing them. At a proprietors' meeting at Concord,

Nov. 1, 1737, the contract was confirmed; and they "voted and granted to said Sheldon, his heirs and assigns, for ever, eighty acres of land, to be by him laid out in one or two places, in a regular form, in any of the common land in the township, excepting the land reserved on account of the mine; the land drowned by his mill-dam to be accounted a part of the eighty acres: provided that there be not more than twenty acres of meadow included in said pond, and eighty acres of land; provided also he keep up a saw-mill and grist-mill in said township, according to his obligation and agreement made with him."

But Mr. Sheldon never built the mills. At a meeting of the proprietors at Concord, Sept. 6, 1739, it was "voted that the Committee chosen to agree about mills in said township be directed, as soon as may be, to procure some suitable person or persons to build a good saw-mill and corn-mill in said township, and to give them such encouragement in any of the common lands or streams within said township as they can or may agree for; and to enter into obligation for the same, in the name of the proprietors." "Also voted that the Committee chosen to let out the mills in said township be fully empowered to put Mr. Samuel Sheldon's bond in prosecution as soon as may be; or the Committee may have a liberty to agree with Mr. Sheldon as they see fit."

A proprietors' meeting was warned to assemble in Concord, Sept. 16, 1742; and one article in the warrant was in these words, — "to inquire whether there is a saw-mill erected in said township, or like to be." On this article the following action is recorded: "Inquired, and there is no mill erected." About three weeks after, at an adjournment of the meeting, the Committee about the mills were instructed to put Mr. Sheldon's bond in suit. At this time, no place had been fixed upon for the location of the mill. In August, 1743, the proprietors refused to give up Mr. Sheldon's bond. It seems, however, never to have been actually sued. At this meeting, in 1743, the proprietors purchased Mr. Thomas Hobbs's right in the township, to secure the forty-acre lot already assigned to him, in order that they might use it for a mill-privilege. This was lot No. 91. The water-privilege, it is said, was the one now occupied by Messrs. Greenwood, Jennison and Co. The purchase included not only the forty-acre lot, but also one share in all the lands then undivided, amounting to upwards of a hundred and fifty acres more. The price allowed to Mr. Hobbs was £26. 10s., to be paid in twelve months, without interest. The proprietors' books do not contain any record of the contract for building the saw-mill on this location. But it appears that a bargain was made with Lieut. James Simonds, Reuben Richardson, and Oliver Richardson. Most likely, it was agreed to give them the land in consideration of building the mill. Probably, it was erected in the course of the autumn of 1743. In November, 1743, a Committee was chosen "to clear the road from the meeting-house place to the saw-mill in said township, and also to look out and mark a road from said mill, across Otter River, into Narraganset No. 2." At that time, there were no permanent habitations here. The next year, 1744, the Indian hostilities commenced, as elsewhere described. No settlers came in for about seven years; and the saw-mill was probably neglected. Upon the return of peace in 1749, it was not in a condition for use; and the clerk was directed to notify Lieut. Simonds and his partners "to rectify the mill, so that it may be in order for sawing, and for the benefit of the township; so that they may fulfil their contract." In May, 1755, the proprietors chose a Committee "to take care of the saw-mill, and see that the owners perform according to contract." In March, 1756, on an article "to see whether the proprietors will build a new saw-mill in the township," it "passed in the negative." Another mill, however, was built not long after; for in March, 1760, there was an article "to see if the propriety will choose a Committee to deal with the partners in the *old* saw-mill, for neglect;" but "it passed in the negative."

In May, 1753, it was voted "to build a corn-mill." A tax of six shillings on each right was laid the same year for that purpose, amounting to a hundred and twenty dollars. Mr. Thomas Sawyer built the grist-mill, in 1754, "on Otter River." It appears that he was to own the mill, and receive a sum of money, in consideration of building it, and engaging to do grinding. In 1763, the proprietors, who still met and acted as a corporation for some purposes, notwithstanding the incorporation of the town of Templeton, had an article in a warrant for a meeting, "to see if the proprietors will prosecute in law the bond against Thomas Sawyer, for his not grinding according to contract for the inhabitants of said town; or to act thereon as said proprietors shall think proper." It was voted to choose a Committee to see that Thomas Sawyer fulfil his contract with respect to the mill. No further notice of the subject appears in the records afterwards.

ROADS.

A very large proportion of the expenditures of this town, from the beginning, have been for making and repairing roads. It would not be practicable, within any moderate limits, for us to give an account of the many locations of highways which appear on the records. Little was done towards making roads till after permanent settlers had come in subsequent to 1750. In 1737, a Committee was paid £18. 4s. (in old-tenor currency, at that time equal to about a fourth of the same amount lawful money) for "marking and clearing a road to the township." This probably meant no more than marking out a sort of bridle-path from Westminster. In 1740, a road was "marked and cleared from Narraganset No. 2 to Pequoiage." "A bridge," at the cost of nine pounds (old tenor), was built in 1741 or 1742.

In October, 1742, it was voted "to clear a road to all the settlers' lots, *fit for passing on horseback;* and also to Nichewog (Petersham), from the corner of this township; and also a road to the mill-place, wherever it shall be." Under this vote, and another authorizing a road to Narraganset No. 2, about forty days' work was paid for. The "settlers" were not yet here: probably a road was cleared of trees to Westminster, and perhaps to Petersham. In 1750, the proprietors granted a tax "for roads through the township, and also to Nichewog line and Pequoiage line," amounting to eighty dollars in the whole. That sum was sufficient, according to the scale of prices adopted in 1753 for highway-work, to pay for a man and a pair of oxen a hundred and fifteen days. In 1752, it was voted that "three rods shall be the general measure for width for the roads through the township; and, in difficult places, to be left discretionary with the Committee as to width." In 1753, the Committee chosen to lay out new roads were directed not to lay them out "before the settlers have pitched on their house-spots."

The expenses in this town for bridges have not been very large. In 1763, the town-record says, "Mr. Noah Merritt undertook to build a bridge over Otter River for ten pounds; and the town granted it to him, and chose a Committee to see that the work is done according to bargain." This was "on the road to Ipswich-Canada" (Winchendon). The bridge over Otter River, at the Factory Village, seems not to have been built till 1778. It was then called "the bridge between Leonard Stone's and Timothy Haild's."

The method of repairing highways, till within a few years, has always, with the exception of the year 1832, been by a tax which was allowed to be worked out by the persons assessed, under the supervision of the highway-surveyors. For many years, the price allowed was about fifty cents a day for a man, and twenty-five cents for a pair of oxen. In 1787, the price allowed was fourpence an hour for a man "for work faithfully performed," and half as much for a yoke of oxen and cart or plough. The price continued the same till 1795, when it was raised one quarter for both men and ox-work. In 1796, the price was raised to sixpence per hour for men, and threepence for cart and oxen. Since 1850, the method has been changed; and all highway-taxes in this town are now paid in money.

Till within recent times, it was customary for the people in winter, when the roads were obstructed by snow, to volunteer to break them out, and no charge was made to the town. This is now done by the highway-surveyors, at the town's expense.

PROCEEDINGS FOR THE SETTLEMENT AND THE DISMISSION OF REV. MR. POND.

At a proprietors' meeting, Oct. 2, 1754, the records say,—

> Voted and chose with unanimity Mr. Daniel Pond to settle in the work of the gospel ministry in the township; and also voted to add to the General Court's encouragement, as his settlement, if he should accept the call to settle as aforesaid, the sum of fifty-five pounds, lawful money; the one half to be paid in six months after his ordination, and the other half to be paid at the expiration of one year after said term. Voted that we give the said Mr. Daniel Pond fifty-five pounds, lawful money, per annum, as a salary for the first three years after his ordination, and that the sum of fifty-three pounds be his annual support after that term, in case he accepts the call, and settles in the work of the ministry in this place; and also voted that the Rev. Mr. Aaron Whitney be desired to carry a copy of these votes to Mr. Pond, and desire him to comply therewith.

The meeting was twice adjourned to receive Mr. Pond's answer, which was read and accepted by vote at a meeting, Dec. 11, 1754.

The answer was in these words:—

To the Proprietors of Narraganset Township No. 6, at their Meeting by repeated adjournments from Oct. 2, 1754, to Dec. 11 ensuing.

GENTLEMEN, — I received, by the hand of the Rev. Mr. Aaron Whitney, a copy of your votes passed at your meeting on Oct 2, as before mentioned, respecting my settling among you in the capacity of a gospel minister; and in answer thereto, in the first place, I return you my hearty thanks for your notice of me, and good-will expressed towards me, notwithstanding my unworthiness, &c. Further: after some deliberation and advice on said affair, esteeming it of signal importance, I accept the call given me to the work of the gospel ministry in this place; and if it should please God, in his all-disposing providence, to order my ordination to the pastoral office here, I hope, by his Spirit and grace, I shall be enabled, in some good measure, to fulfil my ministry.

So I remain your servant in Christ Jesus,

DANIEL POND.

Having accepted this answer, the proprietors voted that the Rev. Aaron Whitney, of Petersham, Mr. Jason Whitney, and Mr. Hezekiah Whitcomb, "be a Committee to transact all affairs relating to the ordination of Mr. Daniel Pond, so far forth as it concerns this propriety."

Very soon after, however, in consequence of the hostilities which had commenced between the English and the French, there were alarms of Indian incursions in this neighborhood; and it appears that nothing was done about Mr. Pond's ordination for ten months after his acceptance. But at a proprietors' meeting, Oct. 15, 1755, it was voted "that the Committee forthwith proceed to the ordination." Having consulted with Mr. Pond, the Committee appointed the second Wednesday of December for that purpose.

An Ecclesiastical Council accordingly assembled on that day, and completed the organization of the church here, and ordained Mr. Pond, as appears from the following certificate: —

This may certify whom it may concern, that the churches hereafter mentioned — viz., the churches of New Salem, Petersham, and Narraganset No. 2 * — met on the tenth day of December,

---

* These churches were represented by Rev. Mr. Kendall, pastor at New Salem, Rev. Aaron Whitney, pastor at Petersham, and Rev. Elisha Marsh, pastor at Westminster (then called Narraganset, No. 2), and their respective delegates. — See Church Records.

1755, at Narraganset No. 6, and, after forming into a council, did gather a church, set apart and ordain the Rev. Mr. Daniel Pond the first minister of that plantation.

Attest, SAMUEL KENDALL,
Moderator.

ENTERTAINMENT OF GUESTS AT REV. MR. POND'S ORDINATION.

The Committee supplied the following provisions and other articles for a public entertainment of those who came to attend the ordination of Rev. Mr. Pond. The bills were paid by the proprietors. Most of the items were computed in the "old-tenor" currency, which at the time was depreciated, compared with "lawful money," so that a pound old tenor was worth no more than two shillings eightpence; in other words, in the ratio of seven and a half for one. The prices are here reduced, as nearly as practicable, from the old-tenor rates, in pounds, shillings, and pence, to the equivalent sums in dollars and cents: —

15½ lbs. beef, at 2¾ cts. per lb.	$0.43
37½ lbs. pork, at 4½ cts. per lb.	1.69
50 lbs. veal, at 2¼ cts. per lb.	1.12
A pair of geese, 14½ lbs., at 2¼ cts. per lb.	0.32
4 hens, at 8 cts. per hen	0.32
5 pecks wheat-flour	1.00
10 lbs. cheese, at 6½ cts. per lb.	0.65
10½ lbs. butter, at 9 cts. per lb.	0.94
1 nutmeg	0.06
Allspice and pepper	0.09
9 lbs. sugar, at 12 cts. per lb.	1.08
4 lbs. raisins, at 10 cts. per lb.	0.40
1 lb. chocolate, at 27 cts. per lb.	0.27
1 peck malt, at 11 cts. per peck	0.11
1 bush. apples, at 9 cts. per bush.	0.09
1 bl. cider, at $1 per bl.	1.00
7¾ galls. rum, at 55 cts. per gall.	4.25
½ gall. West-India rum, at 88 cts. per gall.	0.44
7⅓ lbs. tobacco, at 6⅔ cts. per lb.	0.49
3 doz. pipes, at 5 cts. per doz.	0.15
1½ bush. oats, at 20 cts. per bush.	0.30

The following bills of expense for the ordination were also paid out of the proprietors' treasury: —

Mr. Phinehas Byam's Account.

NARRAGANSET No. 6, Dec. 12, 1755.

	s.	d.
To keeping horses belonging to Mr. Pond's company, fifteen days in all	8	0
To the Council's horses, two for one day	1	0
and three horses part of a day	1	0
To bread to value of	1	4
To meat 10 lbs., at 2d. per lb.	1	8
To my trouble in making seats in the meeting-house, &c.	2	8
	15	8

PHINEHAS BYAM.

Mr. Zaccheus Barrett's Account.

NARRAGANSET No. 6, Dec. 9, 1755.

	s.	d.
To keeping two horses, each one day	1	1
To keeping three horses, each four days	6	5
To riding after a kettle	2	0
To carting boards to the meeting-house from Mr. Cobleigh's and back	3	0
To entertaining Mr. Pond's company; viz., four men, three meals each	6	5
	18	11

ZACCHEUS BARRETT.

Among the items furnished for the ordination occasion appears "one pound of chocolate." This was a favorite article with Rev. Mr. Pond; and it may be presumed that the hostess, Mrs. Whitney, understood how to prepare it better than did Mrs. Byam, in whose family Mr. Pond boarded. The anecdote, according to tradition, is, that Mr. Pond, one Sunday morning, told Mrs. Byam (wife of Jacob Byam, whose residence was at the place where now stands the house of Capt. Stephen S. Maynard) that he should like some chocolate after the close of the public services, and gave her a cake of the article. The good woman had never seen such a thing before, and felt a slight distrust of her ability to prepare it, but, like many others, was unwilling to confess a want of knowledge. So she bravely promised to have it ready. But, on Mr. Pond's return in the afternoon, the usual dinner was produced, — "a boiled dish," — but no chocolate. With disconsolate face and many regrets, she assured him she did not know how it happened: "Certainly, when the vegetables were put into the pot to boil, I put in the chocolate too; for I meant to boil it about as long as the other things. I have taken every thing out carefully; but nothing can I find of *that* anywhere."

COPY OF THE WARRANT AND PROCEEDINGS OF THE MEETINGS FOR REV. MR. POND'S DISMISSION.

WORCESTER, SS. — Application therefor being made to me, the subscriber, by a sufficient number of the proprietors of the Narraganset township No. 6, — these are therefore in his majesty's name to warn said proprietors to meet at the meeting-house in said township on the last Tuesday of July next, at nine o'clock in the morning, to act on the following articles; viz., First (it having pleased Almighty God to permit an unhappy difference to arise between the pastor, church, and flock in this plantation, which occasioned the appointment of an Ecclesiastical Council to sit among them on the last Tuesday of July next), to vote and act on the advice and directions we shall receive from said Council as they shall think proper. Art. 2d. To see if the proprietors will grant money for defraying the expenses of said Council. — Given under my hand and seal, at Narraganset No. 6, this twenty-seventh day of June, *anno Domini* 1759, and in the thirty-third year of his majesty's reign.

CHARLES BAKER,
Proprietors' Clerk.

A meeting was held accordingly July 31, and adjourned from morning to afternoon, then to the evening, and to the next day, and again till evening, and to the morning of the third day. "The aforesaid several adjournments," the record says, "were to wait for the result of the Ecclesiastical Council then sitting in said township." The third morning, impatient, apparently, of the delay, the meeting was dissolved. But, during the third day, the Council finished their deliberations; and, a few days after, another proprietors' meeting was warned to assemble Sept. 12, with an article "to see if the proprietors will agree to what the Ecclesiastical Council have done with respect to Mr. Daniel Pond's dismission." On this article, it was voted "that Mr. Daniel Pond be dismissed according to the result of the Ecclesiastical Council held here Aug. 2, 1759." Mr. Pond seems to have ceased to officiate immediately after the decision of the Council. The proceedings and result of this Council are not recorded, either on the books of the proprietors or the Church Records. Probably the minutes were retained by the scribe of the Council; and nothing remains to show what pastors and churches were present to compose it.

At the meeting, Sept. 12, Mr. Jonas Wilder, Rev. Aaron Whitney (of Petersham), and Mr. Abraham Knowlton, were chosen "a Committee to provide preaching in said township."

GROUND-PLAN OF THE FIRST MEETING-HOUSE.

EAST.

NORTH. — Fifty feet.

FISK HOWE.

COOPER SAWYER.

FLETCHERS.

Dea. PAUL KENDALL.

Pulpit.

Deacons' Seat.

Rev. Mr. SPARHAWK.

BENJAMIN READ, Esq.

EBENEZER GOODRICH.

JOSHUA WRIGHT.

E. FRENCH and D. UPHAM.

L. HOWE, MRS. TUCKER, and SIMEON HORTON.

Stairs to Gallery.

OLD PEOPLE.

Women's Side.

LOVELL WALKER, Esq.

Dea. CUTTING.

ISRAEL LAMB.

Dr. JOSIAH HOWE.

Capt. TURNER.

Capt. STONE.

FREE SEATS FOR

Men's Side.

SIMON STONE.

Capt. COOK.

Mr. WILKINSON.

ADAM JONES.

Capt. RICHARDSON.

Esq. FISHER.

HEZEKIAH HANCOCK and JONA. WHITCOMB.

ZACCHEUS BARRETT and JAMES DOLBEAR.

ARTEMAS HOWE and WILLIAM RICE.

Front Double Doors.

SOUTH.

Captain ORCUTT.

O. HUNT and THOS. BURRAGE.

Deacon WILDER.

Stairs to Gallery.

Mr. FITTS and JOS. HASKELL.

JABEZ BUSH and JONA. HORTON.

SAMUEL BAKER and ZEBEDEE SIMONDS.

WEST. — Forty feet.

The above nearly represents the ground-plan of the old meeting-house and its pews, as it was towards the close of Rev. Mr. SPARHAWK's ministry.

PLAN OF THE GALLERIES IN THE FIRST MEETING-HOUSE.

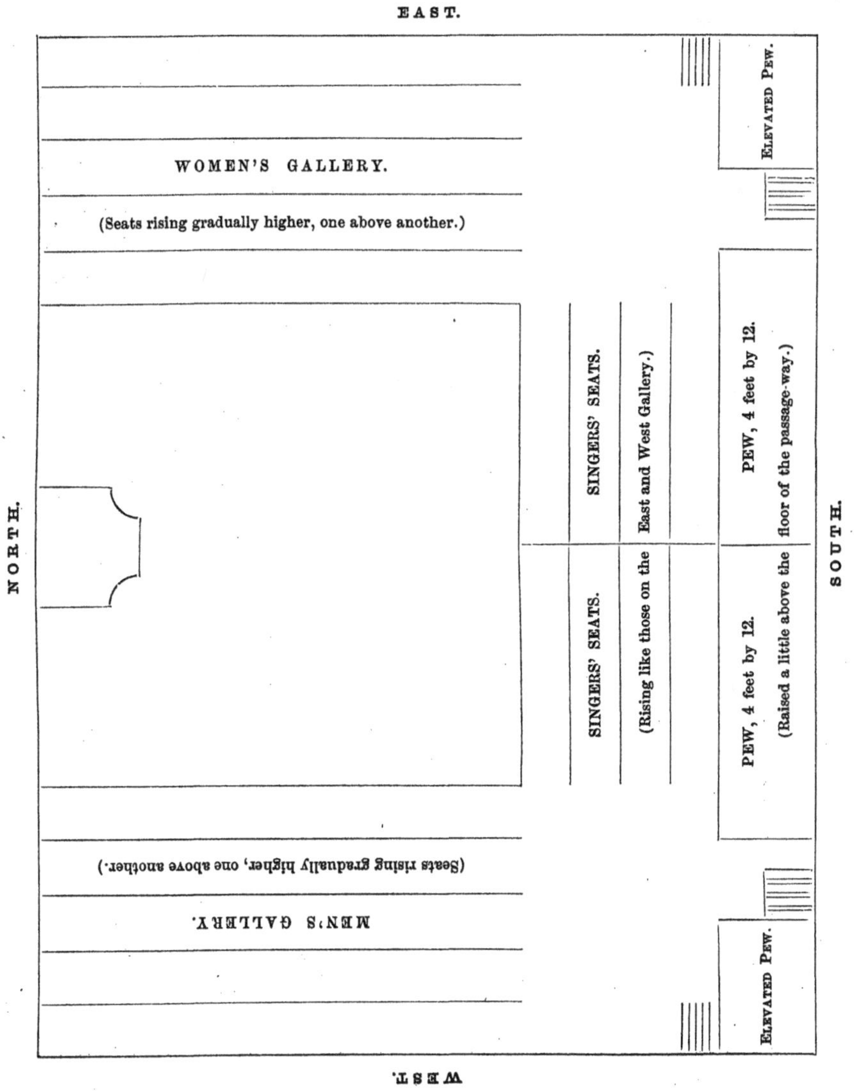

EAST.

WOMEN'S GALLERY.

(Seats rising gradually higher, one above another.)

ELEVATED PEW.

SINGERS' SEATS.

SINGERS' SEATS.

(Rising like those on the East and West Gallery.)

PEW, 4 feet by 12.

PEW, 4 feet by 12.

(Raised a little above the floor of the passage-way.)

NORTH.

SOUTH.

MEN'S GALLERY.

(Seats rising gradually higher, one above another.)

ELEVATED PEW.

WEST.

At the time of Rev. Mr. Sparhawk's ordination, there was only one pew erected in the meeting-house: it was adjoining the pulpit-stairs, and was given to Mr. Sparhawk by a vote passed at a meeting of the proprietors. As the meeting-house had been built by a tax on the proprietors' lands, and not upon the polls or personal property of the inhabitants, it was considered just that the privilege of having pews should belong to the proprietors. Accordingly they voted, at a meeting held Nov. 30, 1763, "first, that we will proceed to the disposing of the pew-ground in the meeting-house; secondly, that John Whitcomb, Esq., have one pew in the meeting-house, equal to others in general; thirdly, that those proprietors that have the most lands in Templeton draw the other pews, they *building them*, and ceiling the meeting-house from the lower floor to the bottom of the windows, and casing them, — they doing the ceiling in eight months, and building their pews in twenty months from this day; and, upon the non-performance of these conditions, each person failing therein to forfeit his pew to the use of the town."

A Committee allotted a tier of *pew-spaces* around the wall of the house to eighteen proprietors. After these pews were built, the central space within was filled up with ranges of long seats, occupied by women on the east side of the middle aisle, and by men on the west side. At various times during the next forty years, the central spaces were disposed of for pews, with the exception of two rows of the long free-seats, — the ones nearest the pulpit. The galleries were occupied with free-seats. In 1770, however, it was voted that Samuel Wilder, Edmond Stone, Joseph Osgood, and Abner Miles, "for their rights in the meeting-house, may build two pews, one over each pair of gallery-stairs, so high up as not to discommode the travelling up stairs nor up to the seats." Two other long pews (or four short ones), in the gallery, back of the singers, were afterwards disposed of. No other pews were ever erected in the galleries. In 1766, it was voted "to let Mr. Nathaniel

Holman and Mr. James Peirce make windows in their pews, upon their own cost, and so as to leave the meeting-house decent." For many years, the larger portion of the congregation occupied the long free-seats before spoken of. The place each one was to occupy was determined by a Committee appointed by the town to "seat the meeting-house." The seats of most dignity, or those considered most eligible, were assigned to the largest tax-payers; and so on in a graduated order throughout. The town first appointed such a Committee in 1765. The duty was a somewhat delicate and difficult one. To say nothing of other points that might arise, it was a question of some moment, to be settled at the outset, as to what the order of the several seats actually was in point of "dignity." Not wishing to take too much responsibility on themselves, the Committee asked the town (an article for the purpose being inserted into the town-meeting warrant) "*to dignify the seats;*" that is, determine their relative rank. But the article "passed in the negative;" and so the Committee had to do it themselves. Another Committee "seated the meeting-house" in 1770; and the process was repeated in 1778 and in 1797. Throughout Mr. Sparhawk's ministry, it was customary for the whole congregation to remain in their places, after the close of the services, till the minister had left the pulpit and passed out of the house. In 1765, the town directed that "the people move out of the seats, after divine service, according to the dignity of the seats, one seat at a time."

Over the minister's head was the "sounding-board," formerly so common. Directly before the pulpit, and facing the congregation, was the "deacons' seat." As long as the old meeting-house stood, those who held that office always occupied, during the service of public worship, the seat mentioned. There are many still living who recollect the venerable forms of Deacon BYAM, Deacon WILDER, and Deacon KENDALL, as they appeared occupying that position from Sunday to Sunday, half a century ago.

The first meeting-house was long left unpainted; they could not afford the expense: but the Building Committee were instructed "to see that the *doors* and *windows* are handsomely colored." Soon after the incorporation of the town, an appropriation was made of fifty pounds "towards finishing the meeting-house." Extensive repairs were made between 1785 and 1792. It was then, for the first time, voted to paint it, — to be "of the color of Leominster."

INSCRIPTION ON REV. MR. SPARHAWK'S GRAVESTONE.

A horizontal slab is placed over Rev. Mr. Sparhawk's grave, which is near the meeting-house. The following is a copy of the inscription: —

This Monument

IS RAISED

TO THE MEMORY OF THE REVEREND, LEARNED, AND PIOUS

EBENEZER SPARHAWK, A.M.,

Pastor of the Congregational Church, Templeton,

Who expired Nov. 25, A.D. 1805, in the sixty-eighth year of his age, and forty-fifth of his ministry.

Early in life, he devoted himself to the service of his God and Saviour.

Endued with good powers of mind, improved by education, and sanctified by grace, he proved a burning and shining light.

In the pulpit he was clear and pungent, rightly dividing the Word.

In the circle of his acquaintance he was ever a welcome guest, his conversation being ever pleasant and improving.

From a child he knew the Holy Scriptures, and was mighty in them.

In faith he was sound and evangelical; in rectitude, pure and exemplary.

A strict adherence to the order and discipline of the churches was a distinguishing trait in his character.

As a Husband he was affectionate; as a Father, tender.

He ruled his own house well; and his children arise up and call him blessed.

With assiduity and fidelity he persevered in his work, until called to receive his reward.

The sun shall cease to shine, and stars shall fade away, and earth and time grow old and die; but his virtues shall live:

and the eye of faith and charity now beholds him walking high in salvation and the climes of bliss.

BURYING-PLACES. — PUBLIC COMMON.

In 1754, two burial-places were laid out by the proprietors of the township, — one at the site of the meeting-house, and one at the west part of the township. The latter was to contain one acre; and land belonging to Thomas Drury was taken for the purpose, and other land allowed him as a substitute. Mr. Drury was paid thirteen shillings and fourpence for clearing the lot. At the meeting-house, the burial-place was laid out, together with land for a common, eight acres and seventy rods in the whole. William Fletcher was the first person buried in it.

The survey of this land, made Jan. 29, 1759, is recorded in vol. i. of the Proprietors' Records, p. 37. One of the bounds then was a beech-tree; another, a hemlock-tree; another, a maple-tree; another, a chestnut-stump. Some difficulty arising about the boundary between this lot and Mr. Abner Newton's land, the proprietors, November, 1758, authorized their Committee to adjust it by giving or receiving deeds. (Proprietors' Records, vol. ii. pp. 18, 19.) In 1759, Abner Newton was paid "for clearing the Common by the meeting-house." In 1763, the Common was further cleared of trees and stumps.

At a proprietors' meeting, May 3, 1786, when the affairs of that corporation were being drawn towards a close, a vote was passed to confirm to the town of Templeton this grant of the burying-place and Common. In 1814 and 1816, votes were passed by the town to authorize the purchase of land to enlarge the north part of the Common. In 1795, the town voted "to fence the burying-ground, and have the walls handsomely topped off." At various times, the town authorized the Selectmen to make repairs, and provide for the care of the burial-place.

In 1850, the town purchased the large lots now used — one at Baldwinville, and one near the Centre — for new burial places. They are admirably suited, by natural adaptation, to the purpose. Successful efforts have already been made by individuals to commence the ornamenting of these grounds; and it is to be hoped they will indeed become attractive and fitting places to be associated with the hallowed memories of the departed. May all good citizens do their part in the work!

COPY OF THE ACT OF INCORPORATION OF THE TOWN.

ANNO REGNI TERTII, [L.S.] REGIS GEORGII SECUNDO.

An Act for incorporating the Plantation called Narraganset No. 6, in the County of Worcester, into a Town by the Name of Templetown.

Whereas the plantation of Narraganset No. 6, lying in the county of Worcester, is competently filled with inhabitants who labor under great difficulties and inconveniences by means of their not being a town; therefore —

Be it enacted by the Governor, Council, and House of Representatives, That the said plantation, commonly called and known by the name of Narraganset No. 6, bounding westerly on Poquioge, southerly on Rutland District and Petersham, easterly on Westminster, northerly on Ipswich-Canada and Royalshire, be, and hereby is, erected into a town by the name of Templetown; and that the said town be, and hereby is, invested with all the powers, privileges, and immunities that any of the towns of this province do or may by law enjoy; —

Provided that nothing in this Act shall be so understood or construed as in any measure to supersede or make void any grants or assessments already made or agreed on by the proprietors of said place in time past, but that the same shall remain and be as effectual as if this Act had not been made.

And be it further enacted, That Joshua Willard, Esq., be, and hereby is, empowered to issue his warrants to some principal inhabitant of the said plantation, requiring him, in his majesty's name, to warn and notify the said inhabitants qualified to vote in town-affairs, that they meet together at such time and place in said plantation as by said warrant shall be appointed, to choose such officers as may be necessary to manage the affairs of said town; and the inhabitants, being so met, shall be, and hereby are, empowered to choose said officers accordingly.

Feb. 23, 1762. — This Bill, having been read three several times in the House of Representatives, passed to be enacted.

JAMES OTIS, *Speaker*.

Feb. 23, 1762. — This Bill, having been read three several times in Council, passed to be enacted.

March 6, 1762. — By the Governor, I consent to the enacting this Bill. FRA. BERNARD.

It will be noticed that the foregoing Act of Incorporation spells the name Templetown. It is so spelled also in the earliest town-records. But in the Tax Act, passed by the General Court in 1763, it was spelled Templeton. The Selectmen repeatedly called it so in their official papers in 1763. Both ways were used by the Selectmen in the same instrument in a "warning out" in 1765; but after February, 1764, the name was always called Templeton in the town-meeting warrants.

There has been a tradition that the town was so called after "some person" who bore the name of Temple; but whether it was in commemoration of the family of that name celebrated in English history, or for one more obscure in station, is now unknown.

TAXES GRANTED BY THE PROPRIETORS.

While the affairs of the township were managed by the proprietors, from 1732 to 1762, the taxes granted by them, which were laid equally upon each original right, were nearly of the following amounts: —

	£	s.	d.
Various sums, in old-tenor currency, granted before any of the lots were settled, for incidental expenses in procuring the grant, dividing the lands, holding meetings, and for roads, &c., — equal in silver, for each lot, to about	1	0	0

	£	s.	d.
Tax on each "non-settler's" lot, mostly paid to those who did settle, — equal, in lawful money, to about	1	6	8
For highways	3	10	8
For building meeting-house	1	0	0
For supply of pulpit, and for the "settlement" and salaries of Rev. Mr. Pond and Rev. Mr. Sparhawk, before incorporation of town, about	5	0	0
Tax for building grist-mill	0	6	0
Taxes for incidental expenses, at various times, about .	1	1	8

So that the whole amount of taxation on each original share in the township, previous to the incorporation of the town, was not far from £13. 5s., — equal to $44.17.

TAXES IN 1763.

The town-taxes assessed in Templeton in 1763, the next year after its incorporation as a town, amounted, beside the highway-tax, to £25: namely, £15, equal to $50, for schools and town-charges; and £10, equal to $33.33, for building a bridge over Otter River. This sum of £25 was assessed upon about eighty persons. Nearly three-fourths of the amount was laid upon polls, and only about one-quarter on the property. The highest tax to any individual on real estate was four shillings and one penny. The following is a list of the names of the persons taxed: —

John Atwood.
Charles Baker.
Zaccheus Barrett.
Timothy Butterfield.
Jacob Byam.
Phinehas Byam.
Samuel Byam.
Joshua Church.
John Cobleigh.
James Carruth.
John Chamberlin.
John Crossett.
William Crossett.
Reuben Cummings.
Eleazer Davis.
John Death.
Thomas Drury.
Caleb Fletcher.
Joel Fletcher.
Timothy Haild.
Israel Hale.
Stephen Haskell.

Nathaniel Holman.
Nathaniel Holman, jun.
Jonathan Holman.
Joseph Horton.
Ebenezer Horton.
Joseph Kendrick.
Capt. Thomas How.
John How.
Abel Hunt.
Enoch Jewett.
Silas Jones.
Ezekiel Knowlton.
Joshua Lamb.
Dennis Locklin.
Noah Merritt.
John Macklewaine.
George Nicholas.
William Oak.
Seth Oak.
Samuel Osgood.
James Peirce.
Jason Parmenter.
Samuel Rice.
Samuel Ross.
John Richardson.
Israel Richardson.
Abraham Sawyer.
Thomas Sawyer.
Abner Sawyer.
Samuel Sawyer.
Hezekiah Sprague.
Henry Sawtell.
Enoch Sawtell.
John Stuart.
Jeremiah Stuart.
Ephraim Shattuck.
Silas Shattuck.
Levi Sylvester.
Jacob Spaulding.
John Wheeler.
John Wheeler, jun.
Jason Whitney.
Moses Whitney.
Thomas Witt.
Jonas Wilder.
Josiah Wilder.
John Wilder.
Ebenezer Wright.
Joshua Wright.
Job Whitcomb.
Joseph White.
Thomas White.
Benjamin Wesson.

The following persons were also taxed, in 1763, for real estate only; and were therefore probably non-residents: —

David Goddard.
Daniel Goddard.
James Kendall.
James Simonds.

SUMS GRANTED BY THE TOWN, EACH YEAR SINCE ITS INCORPORATION, FOR HIGHWAYS, FOR SCHOOLS, AND FOR TOWN-CHARGES, INCLUDING SPECIAL GRANTS.

Year.	Highways.	Schools.	Town-charges.
1762	£40	£00	£10
1763	40	15 *	10 †

* School and town charges. † For bridge over Otter River.

Year.	Highways.	Schools.	Town-charges.
1764	£50	£10	£6
1765	53	16	12
1766	100	20	13
1767	100	20	10
1768	100	20	6
1769	100	25	20
1770	100	40	6
1771	100	35	42
1772	125	35	36
1773	140	40	40
1774	150	35	30
1775	50	20	0
1776	60	35	30
1777	80	50	45
1778	300 *	60 *	200 *
1779	1,200 *	1,200 *	1,000 *
1780	7,000 †	6,000 *	4,000 *
1781	10,500 ‡	12,000	20,000 §
1782	150	100	50
1783	150	100	00
1784	150	100	00
1785	200	100	00
1786	250	100	30
1787	100	66⅔	140 ‖
1788	150	50	00
1789	150	40	00
1790	150	45	00
1791	150	60	10
1792	150	60	30 ¶
1793	150	60	20
1794	150	60	30
1795	250	75	120
1796	$1,000 **	$267	$800
1797	1,000	270	700
1798	1,000	270	500
1799	1,000	270	500
1800	1,000	270	400
1801	1,000	300	200
1802	1,000	400	150
1803	1,000	400	600

* Nominal. Paper currency depreciated.
† Nominal. 20s. an hour for a man's work.
‡ Nominal. $5 an hour for a man's work.
§ In August, 1781, granted, instead, £350 silver, and £300 silver for the three-years' soldiers.
‖ Of this grant, £120 to build and repair schoolhouses.
¶ And £70 additional for schoolhouses.
** After 1795, the accounts were changed from English to Federal currency.

Year.	Highways.	Schools.	Town-charges.
1804	$1,000	$400	$600
1805	1,000	450	300
1806	1,000	450	200
1807	1,000	450	300
1808	1,000	450	200
1809	1,000	450	200
1810	1,000	450	200
1811	1,000	450	000
1812	1,000	450	500
1813	1,000	450	1,000
1814	1,000	500	600
1815	1,000	550	400
1816	1,000	550	800
1817	1,000	500	1,000
1818	1,000	600	1,100
1819	1,000	600	900
1820	800	550	900
1821	1,000	500	300
1822	1,000	550	500
1823	1,000	550	600
1824	1,200	600	600
1825	1,200	600	600
1826	1,200	600	700
1827	1,000	500	1,800
1828	1,200	500	700
1829	1,200	600	450
1830	1,200	550	550
1831	1,200	600	800
1832	600 *	600	500
1833	1,500	700	500
1834	1,600	700	700
1835	1,500	700	1,075
1836	1,600	954	600
1837	2,000	1,300	1,000
1838	1,500	800 †	1,000
1839	1,500	800 †	1,500
1840	1,500	800 †	1,050
1841	1,500	1,000	2,500 ‡
1842	1,875	1,000	2,700 §
1843	1,800	1,000	3,000 ‖
1844	1,500	1,000	2,500 ‖
1845	1,500	1,000	2,800 ‖

* This grant was assessed to be paid in money.

† For three years, $200 a year was added to the school appropriation; it being the interest on the surplus revenue.

‡ $1,500 of this for new road.

§ $1,700 of this for road and poor-farm debts.

‖ Including payment toward road-debt; about $1,000 a year.

Year.	Highways.	Schools.	Town-charges.
1846	$1,500	$1,000	$3,500 *
1847	1,500	1,000	3,200 *
1848	1,575	1,000	4,000 *
1849	1,500 †	1,300	3,500 *
1850	1,100 ‡	1,300	3,000 *
1851	1,300	1,300	5,000 *
1852	1,400	1,300	3,500 *
1853	1,400	1,500 §	2,500
1854	1,500	1,500	2,800 ‖
1855	1,700	1,500	3,500 ‖
1856	2,000	2,000 ¶	4,000 ‖

SELECTMEN.

The following is a list of the Selectmen of Templeton from the beginning to the present time. From 1762 to 1786, the whole original township was together. In 1786, the town of "Gerry" was set off from Templeton.

1762.
Jason Whitney.
Joshua Hyde.
Abner Newton.

1763.
Nathaniel Holman.
Charles Baker.
Jonas Wilder.

1764.
John Richardson.**
Charles Baker.
Ebenezer Wright.
Jonas Wilder.
Abel Hunt.

1765.
Joshua Church.
Joshua Wright.
Jason Whitney.
Jonathan Holman.
Samuel Sawyer.

1766.
Charles Baker.
Ebenezer Wright.
Abel Hunt.
Jonas Wilder.
Joshua Wright.

---

* Including payment toward road-debt; about $1,000 a year.
† $300 of this in money.
‡ From 1850 to the present time, the highway-taxes have been made payable in money.
§ $141 additional expended for school-apparatus.
‖ From 1854 to 1856, $3,000 additional was assessed each year for the new roads.
¶ $350 granted for High School, beside the $2,000 for the common schools.
** Moses Whitney was elected on the resignation of John Richardson.

1767.
Henry Sawtell.
John Wheeler, jun.
John Death.
Joseph White.
Jonathan Holman.

1768.
Ezekiel Knowlton.
Charles Baker.
Ebenezer Wright.
Silas Jones.
John Wheeler, jun.

1769.
Jonathan Baldwin.
John Cobleigh.
Jonas Wilder.
Charles Baker.
Ebenezer Wright.

1770.
Jonathan Baldwin.
Jonas Wilder.
Josiah Wilder.
Charles Baker.
Ebenezer Wright.

1771.
Jonathan Baldwin.
Samuel Taylor.
John Richardson.
Charles Baker.
Ebenezer Wright.

1772.
Jonathan Baldwin.
John Brigham.
John Richardson.
Thomas White.
John Cobleigh.

1773.
Jonathan Baldwin.
Ebenezer Wright.
Joshua Wright.
Thomas White.
Joel Grout.

1774.
Jonathan Baldwin.
Ebenezer Wright.
Joshua Wright.
Abner Sawyer.
Joel Grout.

1775.
Jonathan Baldwin.
William Sprague.
Thomas White.
Abel Hunt.
Joel Grout.

1776.
Jonathan Baldwin.
Simon Slocomb.
Thomas White.
William Sprague.
Henry Sawtell.

1777.
Jonathan Baldwin.
Silas Cutler.
Abner Sawyer.
Joel Fletcher.
John Wheeler.

1778.
Ebenezer Wright.
Silas Cutler.
Jonathan Jones.
Thaddeus Brown.
Ezekiel Knowlton.

1779.
Silas Cutler.
Jonathan Jones.
Joel Fletcher.
Thomas White.
Ezekiel Knowlton.

1780.
Ebenezer Wright.
Jonathan Jones.
Ezekiel Knowlton.
Thomas White.
Silas Cutler.

1781.
Ebenezer Wright.
Jonathan Jones.
Capt. Ezekiel Knowlton.
Thomas White.
Silas Cutler.

1782.
Silas Cutler.
Joel Grout.
Simon Stone.
Gardner Maynard.
Josiah Wilder.

1783.
Ebenezer Wright.
Charles Baker.
Samuel Cook.
Jonathan Stratton.
Deacon Paul Kendall.

1784.
Ebenezer Wright.
Charles Baker.
Samuel Cook.
Jonathan Stratton.
Deacon Paul Kendall.

1785.
Ebenezer Wright.
Charles Baker.
Samuel Cook.
Jonathan Stratton.
Deacon Paul Kendall.

1786.
Ebenezer Wright.
Charles Baker.
Samuel Cook.
Jonathan Stratton.
Deacon Paul Kendall.

1787.
Ebenezer Wright.
Deacon Paul Kendall.
Jonathan Baldwin.
Capt. John Richardson.
Capt. Josiah Wilder.

1788.
Joshua Wright.
Joel Fletcher.
Samuel Cook.
Simon Stone.
Moses Holbrook.

1789.
Ebenezer Wright.
Joel Fletcher.
Jotham Sawyer.
Simon Stone.
Aholiab Sawyer.

1790.
Ebenezer Wright.
Jotham Sawyer.
Timothy Parker.
Samuel Cook.
Capt. Leonard Stone.

1791.
Silas Hazelton.
Leonard Stone.
Silas Cutler.
Aholiab Sawyer.
Simon Stone.

1792.
Silas Hazelton.
Silas Cutler.
Leonard Stone.
Aholiab Sawyer.
Simon Stone.

1793.
Silas Hazelton.
Silas Cutler.
Leonard Stone.
Aholiab Sawyer.
Silas Church.

1794.
Silas Hazelton.
Silas Cutler.
Leonard Stone.
Aholiab Sawyer.
Silas Church.

1795.
Joshua Wright.
Leonard Stone.
Aholiab Sawyer.
Thomas Fisher.
William Goodell.

1796.
Joshua Wright.
Silas Cutler.
Leonard Stone.
Thomas Fisher.
Silas Church.

1797.
Joshua Wright.
Silas Cutler.
Thomas Fisher.
Stephen Bush.
Joseph Balcomb.

1798.
Thomas Fisher.
Joseph Balcomb.
Stephen Bush.
Eden Baldwin.
James Dolbear.

1799.
Thomas Fisher.
Eden Baldwin.
Stephen Bush.
Dr. Josiah Howe.
Jonathan Orcutt.

1800.
Benjamin Read.
Leonard Stone.
Silas Church.
Eden Baldwin.
Stephen Knowlton.

1801.
Thomas Fisher.
Silas Cutler.
Silas Church.
Cooper Sawyer.
Timothy Parker.

1802.
Thomas Fisher.
Silas Cutler.
Cooper Sawyer.
Asa Turner.
David Cobleigh.

1803.
Thomas Fisher.
Silas Cutler.
Cooper Sawyer.
Asa Turner.
David Cobleigh.

1804.
Dr. Josiah Howe.
Sylvanus Howe.
Moses Wright.
Silas Church.
Aaron Jones, jun.

1805.
Dr. Josiah Howe.
Thomas Fisher.
Moses Wright.
Leonard Stone.
Cooper Sawyer.

1806.
Leonard Stone.
Cooper Sawyer.
Stephen Bush.
Eleazer Davis.
Jonathan Holman.

1807.
Moses Wright.
Stephen Bush.
Dr. Josiah Howe.
Lovell Walker.
Eleazer Davis.

1808.
Moses Wright.
Adam Jones.
Elisha Cook.
Leonard Stone.
Jonathan Orcutt.

1809.
Moses Wright.
Adam Jones.
Thomas Fisher.
Jonathan Orcutt.
Asa Turner.

1810.
Moses Wright.
Adam Jones.
Thomas Fisher.
Jonathan Orcutt.
Asa Turner.

1811.
Moses Wright.
David Cobleigh.
Cooper Sawyer.
Aaron Jones.
Cyrus Brown.

1812.
Moses Wright.
David Cobleigh.
Cooper Sawyer.
Aaron Jones.
Joshua Richardson.

1813.
Samuel Cutting.
David Cobleigh.
Cooper Sawyer.
Dr. Josiah Howe.
Ephraim Stone.

1814.
John W. Stiles.
David Cobleigh.
Moses Wright.
Aaron Fiske.
Ephraim Stone.

1815.
John W. Stiles.
Samuel Cutting.
Eden Baldwin.
Cooper Sawyer.
Elisha Cook.

1816.
Moses Wright.
Samuel Cutting.
Col. Leonard Stone.
Aaron Fiske.
Ezekiel Partridge.

1817.
Moses Wright.
Joshua Richardson.
Leonard Stone.
Cooper Sawyer.
Paul Kendall, jun.

1818.
Joshua Richardson.
David Cobleigh.
Ephraim Stone.

1819.
Eden Baldwin.
Simeon Merritt.
Levi Norcross.
Gillam Wilder.
Samuel Cutting.

1820.
Eden Baldwin.
Leonard Stone.
Cooper Sawyer.
Simeon Merritt.
Levi Norcross.

1821.
Eden Baldwin.
Leonard Stone.
Cooper Sawyer.
Simeon Merritt.
Levi Norcross.

1822.
Eden Baldwin.
Leonard Stone.
Cooper Sawyer.
Levi Norcross.
Dr. Josiah Howe.

1823.
Eden Baldwin.
Leonard Stone.
Cooper Sawyer.
Levi Norcross.
William Brown.

1824.
Leonard Stone.
Eleazer Davis.
Cooper Sawyer.
Levi Norcross.
Moses Leland.

1825.
Eleazer Davis.
Moses Leland.
Ephraim Stone.
Elisha Cook.
Samuel Dadman.

1826.
Samuel Dadman.
Elisha Cook.
Joseph Jackson.
John Sawyer.
Joshua Sawyer.

1827.
Ephraim Stone.
Leonard Stone.
Joshua Richardson.
Joshua W. Whitcomb.
Samuel Lee.

1828.
Ephraim Stone.
Leonard Stone.
Joshua Richardson.
Joshua W. Whitcomb.
Samuel Lee.

1829.
Leonard Stone.
Joshua Richardson.
Samuel Lee.
Cooper Sawyer.
Daniel Norcross.

1830.
Ephraim Stone.
Leonard Stone.
Cooper Sawyer.
Joseph Upham.
George W. Jones.

1831.
Samuel Lee.
Artemas Lee.
John Sawyer 2d.
Calvin Townsley.
Joseph Upham.

1832.
Ephraim Stone.
Samuel Lee.
John Sawyer 2d.
Calvin Townsley.
Henry Newton.

1833.
Samuel Dadman.
Calvin Townsley.
Henry Newton.
Moses Leland.
Augustus A. Jones.

1834.
Henry Newton.
Moses Leland.
Augustus A. Jones.
William Graham.
Nathan Farnsworth.

1835.
Ephraim Stone.
William Graham.
Joseph Davis.
Augustus A. Jones.
Nathan Farnsworth.

1836.
Ephraim Stone.
Gilman Day.
Joseph Davis.
Augustus A. Jones.
Nathan Farnsworth.

1837.
Ephraim Stone.
Gilman Day.
Elijah B. Newton.
Augustus A. Jones.
Nathan Farnsworth.

1838.
Joseph Davis.
Stephen S. Maynard.
Elijah B. Newton.
Israel P. Sibley.
Joseph Upham.

1839.
Joseph Davis.
Stephen S. Maynard.
George W. Jones.
Israel P. Sibley.
Charles T. Fisher.

1840.
Jotham Goodnow.
Stephen S. Maynard.
Gilman Day.
Hermon Partridge.
Charles T. Fisher.

1841.
John Sawyer 2d.
Jotham Goodnow.
Samuel Lee.
Thomas Parker.
Lemuel B. Howe.

1842.
Thomas Parker.
Lemuel B. Howe.
Hermon Partridge.
Benjamin Hawkes.
Samuel D. Morley.

1843.
Benjamin Hawkes.
Nathan Farnsworth.
Hermon Partridge.
Joshua Hosmer.
Augustus A. Jones.

1844.
Joshua Hosmer.
Benjamin Hawkes.
John Sawyer 2d.
John W. Work.
Augustus A. Jones.

1845.
Augustus A. Jones.
Benjamin Hawkes.
John Sawyer 2d.
Nathan Farnsworth.
Joshua Sawyer, jun.

1846.
Benjamin Hawkes.
Augustus A. Jones.
Stillman Norcross.
Nathan Farnsworth.
Leonard Stone, jun.

1847.
Benjamin Hawkes.
Augustus A. Jones.
Leonard Stone, jun.

1848.
Benjamin Hawkes.
Augustus A. Jones.
Leonard Stone, jun.
John Sawyer 2d.
Merrick E. Ainsworth.

1849.
John W. Work.
Merrick E. Ainsworth.
John Sawyer 2d.

1850.
Dexter Gilbert.
John W. Work.
James H. Clapp.

1851.
John W. Work.
James H. Clapp.
John Sawyer 2d.

1852.

John W. Work.
James H. Clapp.
John Sawyer 2d.

1853.

John W. Work.
Benjamin Hawkes.
Moses Elliott.
Warren Simonds.
Seth Webb.

1854.
Edward Hosmer.
Benjamin Hawkes.
Moses Elliott.

1855.
Edward Hosmer.*
Benjamin Hawkes.
Otis Warren.

1856.
John Sawyer 2d.
Joshua Sawyer, jun.
George P. Hawkes.

TOWN CLERKS AND TOWN TREASURERS FROM THE BEGINNING TO THE PRESENT TIME.

Year.	Town Clerks.	Town Treasurers.
1762.	Abel Hunt	Zaccheus Barrett.
1763.	Nathaniel Holman	Phinehas Byam.
1764.	John Richardson; removed from town; and Abel Hunt was chosen in his place.	Phinehas Byam.
1765.	Ebenezer Wright	Phinehas Byam.
1766.	Ebenezer Wright	Zaccheus Barrett.
1767.	Ebenezer Wright	Zaccheus Barrett.
1768.	Ebenezer Wright	Phinehas Byam.
1769.	Ebenezer Wright	Phinehas Byam.
1770.	Ebenezer Wright	John Cobleigh.
1771.	Ebenezer Wright	John Cobleigh.
1772.	John Richardson	Abner Sawyer.
1773.	Ebenezer Wright	Abner Sawyer.
1774.	Ebenezer Wright	Abner Sawyer.
1775.	Jonathan Baldwin	Phinehas Byam.
1776.	Simon Slocomb	Phinehas Byam.
1777.	Jonathan Baldwin	Phinehas Byam.
1778.	Ebenezer Wright	Ebenezer French.
1779.	Silas Cutler	Ebenezer French.
1780.	Ebenezer Wright	Ebenezer French.
1781.	Silas Cutler	Phinehas Byam.

* John Sawyer 2d was chosen Selectman after the death of Edward Hosmer.

Year.	Town Clerks.	Town Treasurers.
1782.	Ebenezer Wright	Joshua Wright.
1783.	Ebenezer Wright	Joshua Wright.
1784.	Ebenezer Wright	Joshua Wright.
1785.	Ebenezer Wright	Joshua Wright.
1786.	Ebenezer Wright	Joshua Wright.
1787.	Ebenezer Wright	Jonathan Cutting.
1788.	Joshua Wright	Ebenezer French.
1789.	Ebenezer Wright	Fisk How.
1790.	Ebenezer Wright	Fisk How.
1791.	Silas Hazelton	Fisk How.
1792.	Silas Hazelton	Fisk How.
1793.	Silas Hazelton	Fisk How.
1794.	Silas Hazelton	Fisk How.
1795.	Joshua Wright	Fisk How.
1796.	Joshua Wright	Fisk How.
1797.	Joshua Wright	Silas Hazelton.
1798.	Dr. Josiah Howe	Silas Hazelton.
1799.	Dr. Josiah Howe	James Dolbear.
1800.	Benjamin Read	Thomas Fisher.
1801.	Thomas Fisher	James Dolbear.
1802.	Thomas Fisher	James Dolbear.
1803.	Thomas Fisher	James Dolbear.
1804.	Dr. Josiah Howe	James Dolbear.
1805.	Dr. Josiah Howe	Lovell Walker.
1806.	Moses Wright	Elisha Cook.
1807.	Moses Wright	Elisha Cook.
1808.	Moses Wright	John W. Stiles.
1809.	Moses Wright	John W. Stiles.
1810.	Moses Wright	John W. Stiles.
1811.	Moses Wright	John W. Stiles.
1812.	Moses Wright	John W. Stiles.
1813.	Samuel Cutting	Thomas Fisher.
1814.	John W. Stiles	Thomas Fisher.
1815.	John W. Stiles	Benjamin Read.
1816.	Moses Wright	Benjamin Read.
1817.	Moses Wright	Benjamin Read.
1818.	Moses Wright	Benjamin Read.
1819.	Thomas Fisher	Benjamin Read.
1820.	Thomas Fisher	Benjamin Read.
1821.	Thomas Fisher	Benjamin Read.
1822.	Dr. Josiah Howe	Benjamin Read.
1823.	John Bigelow	Benjamin Read.*
1824.	John Bigelow	Dr. Josiah Howe.
1825.	John Bigelow	Dr. Josiah Howe.
1826.	John Bigelow	Dr. Josiah Howe.
1827.	John Bigelow	Dr. Josiah Howe.

* Edèn Baldwin was elected on the decease of Benjamin Read.

Year.	Town Clerks.	Town Treasurers.
1828.	John Bigelow	Dr. Josiah Howe.
1829.	John Bigelow	John Bigelow.
1830.	John Bigelow	John Bigelow.
1831.	John Bigelow	John Bigelow.
1832.	John Bigelow	John Bigelow.
1833.	John Bigelow	John Bigelow.
1834.	John Bigelow	John Bigelow.
1835.	Thomas J. Waite	John Bigelow.
1836.	Thomas J. Waite	John Bigelow.
1837.	Rufus Wyman	Ephraim Stone.
1838.	Rufus Wyman	Ephraim Stone.
1839.	Rufus Wyman	David Whitcomb.
1840.	Joseph Mason	David Whitcomb.
1841.	Joseph Mason	John W. Work.
1842.	Dexter Gilbert	John W. Work.
1843.	Dexter Gilbert	John W. Work.
1844.	Dexter Gilbert	John W. Work.
1845.	Dexter Gilbert	Dexter Gilbert.
1846.	Dexter Gilbert	Dexter Gilbert.
1847.	Dexter Gilbert	Giles H. Whitney.
1848.	Dexter Gilbert	Joshua Hosmer.
1849.	Dexter Gilbert	Joshua Hosmer.
1850.	Dexter Gilbert	Joshua Hosmer.
1851.	Dexter Gilbert	Joshua Hosmer.
1852.	Dexter Gilbert	David Whitcomb.
1853.	Dexter Gilbert	David Whitcomb.
1854.	Rev. Gerard Bushnell	Giles H. Whitney.
1855.	Rev. Gerard Bushnell	Henry Smith.
1856.	Rev. Gerard Bushnell	Henry Smith.

REPRESENTATIVES TO THE GENERAL COURT.

The town sent no representative to the General Court till the revolutionary strife was drawing near. In 1762, 1765, 1766, and 1767, there was no article in the town-meeting warrants on the subject of sending a representative; and, of course, no action was taken. In each of the other nine years, — from 1762 to 1774, inclusive, — the town voted not to send. Gov. Gage convoked the General Court to meet at Salem, on the 5th of October, 1774, by proclamation dated Sept. 1 of that year. The people of Templeton were already burning with the sentiments of liberty, and opposition to the British aggressions. A town-meeting had been called to assemble on the *25th of August*, the warrant for which had an article, with one clause in these words: "And act upon any other matter relative to the supporting of our charter-rights and liberties as seems most proper." This town-meeting was continued, by successive adjournments, to Sept. 26. On that day, with no other article than the foregoing to support the action, the record says the town "voted to choose a representative." — "Chose Mr. Jonathan Baldwin to represent the town at the Great and General Court to be holden at Salem the present year."

On the 28th of September, Gov. Gage, alarmed by the tokens of public spirit that were everywhere manifested, issued a proclamation declaring his "intention not to meet the said General Court at Salem on the said fifth day of October next," and declaring that the representatives elected to serve at the same were discharged from giving their attendance. But, on the 5th of October, ninety of the representatives thus elected met at Salem. They cautiously waited through that day for the Governor to appear and administer the usual oaths; and then they passed a resolve, ingeniously raising the point, that the Governor's lawful power "to adjourn, prorogue, and dissolve all Great and General Courts doth not take place till after said courts have first *met and convened.*" They therefore claimed that the Governor's proclamation on the 28th of September was a nullity, and resolved that they would act, with other representatives that might be chosen, as a "Provincial Congress." They then adjourned to meet at Concord, and proceeded to exercise the powers of government without leave of Gen. Gage.

Two other Provincial Congresses were formed in 1775: one was convened at Cambridge, Feb. 1, and held two adjourned sessions at Concord and Watertown, and was dissolved May 29; the next met at Watertown, May 31, and was dissolved July 19. To both of these assemblies, Jonathan Baldwin was chosen as delegate from Templeton; viz., at town-meetings on the 4th of January and on the 16th of May.

On the 9th of June, 1775, the Continental Congress, sitting at Philadelphia, passed a resolution, that — no obedience being due "to the act of Parliament for altering the charter of the Colony of Massachusetts Bay, nor to a Governor and Lieut.-Governor who will not observe the directions of, but endeavor to subvert, that charter — the Governor and Lieut.-Governor are to be considered as absent, and their offices vacant." And, in the same resolve, it was recommended to the Provincial Congress of Massachusetts — "as the inconveniences arising from the suspension of the powers of government are intolerable" — "to write letters to the inhabitants of the several places which are entitled to representation in assembly, requesting them to choose such representatives; and that the assembly, when chosen, should elect counsellors, — which assembly and council should exercise the powers of government until a governor of his majesty's appointment will consent to govern the Colony according to its charter." Thus cautiously did the leaders, before independence was declared, take heed not to show *open forms* of rebellion against the king.

In obedience to the directions of the Provincial Congress, issued agreeably to the foregoing recommendations, the Selectmen of Templeton called a town-meeting, July 5, 1775, at which Jonathan Baldwin was again chosen to represent the town "in the Great and General Court to be held at Watertown." And thus for ever passed away the royal authority over us. Since Gov. Gage's time, *no "governor of his majesty's appointment"* has appeared "consenting to govern the Colony" of the Massachusetts Bay. The people hardly realized the magnitude of the change: the constables were posting warrants, just as they had always done, for town-meetings called together by the customary authority of the selectmen; the town-clerks recorded the doings, with no sign that any thing unusual was taking place.

But the warrant for the town-meeting, at which, on the 26th of September, 1774, Jonathan Baldwin was chosen the first representative to the General Court, was issued, requiring the constable, "*in his majesty's name*," "to warn the freeholders and other inhabitants to meet," &c. The *next time* a representative from Templeton was chosen to an assembly, which they ventured to call a "General Court," the warrant no longer makes any mention of "his majesty," but says it is "by order of Congress."

One election, therefore, and one only, has ever been made in Templeton — that of Sept. 26, 1774 — of a representative to a legislature called together by authority of the King of Great Britain through his governor's proclamation. From that day to this, the representatives have been chosen to *the people's* General Court. Their names, and the year of their election, are as follows. Before 1831, the representatives were chosen in May; since, in November.

1775. Jonathan Baldwin.
1776. Capt. John Richardson.
1777. Capt. John Richardson.
1778. Capt. Ezekiel Knowlton.
1779. Capt. Ezekiel Knowlton.
1780. (Voted not to send.)
1781. Capt. Joel Fletcher.
1782. (Voted not to send.)
1783. Capt. Ezekiel Knowlton.
1784. Capt. Ezekiel Knowlton.
1785. Capt. John Richardson.
1786. Jonathan Baldwin.
1787. Capt. Ezekiel Knowlton.
1788. Capt. Ezekiel Knowlton.
1789. Capt. Ezekiel Knowlton.
1790. (Town fined £13 for not sending.)
1791. Capt. Joel Fletcher.
1792. Capt. Joel Fletcher.
1793. Col. Silas Cutler.
1794. (Voted not to send.)
1795. Capt. Leonard Stone.
1796. (Voted not to send.)
1797. Silas Hazelton.
1798. Silas Cutler.
1799. (Voted not to send.)
1800. Leonard Stone.
1801. Leonard Stone.
1802. (Voted not to send.)
1803. Lovell Walker.
1804. (Voted not to send.)
1805. Lovell Walker.
1806. Leonard Stone.
1807. (Voted not to send.)
1808. Lovell Walker.
1809. Leonard Stone.
1810. John W. Stiles.
1811. John W. Stiles.
1812. John W. Stiles.
1813. John W. Stiles.

1814. Moses Wright.
1815. Moses Wright.
1816. Moses Wright.
1817. (Voted not to send.)
1818. (Voted not to send.)
1819. Ephraim Stone.
1820. (Voted not to send.)
1821. (Voted not to send.)
1822. (Voted not to send.)
1823. Benjamin Read.
1824. (Voted not to send.)
1825. Dr. Josiah Howe.
1826. (Voted not to send.)
1827. Dr. Josiah Howe.
1828. Col. Leonard Stone.
1829. Leonard Stone.
1830. Ephraim Stone.
Samuel Lee.
1831.* Leonard Stone.
1832. Artemas Lee.
Samuel Dadman.
1833. Samuel Dadman.
Artemas Lee.
1834. Samuel Dadman.
Artemas Lee.
1835. Samuel Dadman.
1836. Artemas Lee.
1837. Moses Leland.
1838. Moses Leland.
Joseph Davis.
1839. John Boynton.
Moses Leland.
1840. John Boynton.
1841. (Voted not to send.)
1842. Charles T. Fisher.
1843. Charles T. Fisher.
1844. (No choice.)
1845. Gilman Day.
1846. John W. Work.
1847. Artemas Lee.
1848. (No choice.)
1849. John W. Work.
1850. Dexter Gilbert.
1851. John W. Work.
1852. Edward Hosmer.
1853. Benjamin Hawkes.
1854. Frederick Parker.
1855. John Sawyer 2d.
1856. Henry Smith.

CONSTITUTIONAL CONVENTIONS.

The General Court, in 1778, framed a Constitution for Massachusetts; which was submitted to the people, and rejected by a great majority. In Templeton, the vote was twenty-two for, and fifty-one against. The members of the General Court chosen in 1777 were expected to act upon the subject of the Constitution, as well as upon the ordinary subjects. The representative from Templeton that year was Capt. John Richardson.

---

* After the amendment of the State Constitution, ratified in 1830, the representatives were elected in November of each year to serve for the year following.

In 1779 and 1780, a convention of delegates, chosen for the purpose, framed the present Constitution of the State. It was submitted to the people in March, 1780, and adopted by more than two-thirds. In Templeton, May 23, 1780, a committee reported in favor of some amendments; with which suggestions the frame of government was adopted by a vote of fifty-seven to one. It was provided in the Constitution, that, in fifteen years, there might be a convention for revising it. In 1795, the question was submitted to the people, and they voted against holding a convention. In Templeton, the vote was "seventy-six for the Constitution to stand as it is; none against it." It received important amendments proposed by a convention assembled in 1820. In 1853, a convention of delegates was held, and a new constitution prepared; but it was not accepted by the people.

To the convention of 1779–80 were chosen as delegates from Templeton (Jonathan Baldwin having declined) Capt. John Richardson and Mr. Joel Grout. To the convention of 1820, the delegate was Lovell Walker, Esq. To the convention of 1853, the delegate was Gilman Day, Esq.

When the Constitution of the United States was framed, in 1787, it was submitted for ratification, not to the direct votes of the people, but to conventions of delegates in each State. The Massachusetts convention assembled in January, 1788. It consisted of three hundred and sixty members. The majority of these delegates, when they first assembled, were opposed to adopting it as a constitution for the United States; but it was finally ratified in the convention, on behalf of Massachusetts, Feb. 6, 1788, there being a majority of nineteen in its favor.

The delegate from Templeton was Capt. Joel Fletcher.

VOTES FOR GOVERNOR.

The following is a list of the votes for governor in Templeton, each year, from the adoption of the State Constitution in 1780 to 1856. It also shows the comparative strength of the various political parties since the year 1800; the names of the "Federalist" candidates, and subsequently those of the "Whig" party, during its organization, being placed first each year, and the names of the "Democratic" candidates next. Others are specially noted when they occur. The name of the person elected by the people each year is printed in small capitals: —

1780.	No. of Votes.
JOHN HANCOCK	51
James Bowdoin	5

1781.	
JOHN HANCOCK	43
James Bowdoin	1
James Warren	7

1782.	
JOHN HANCOCK	12
James Bowdoin	29
Scattering	6

1783.	
JOHN HANCOCK	37
James Bowdoin	4

1784.	
JOHN HANCOCK	28
James Bowdoin	13
Scattering	4

1785.	
James Bowdoin *	12
Benjamin Lincoln	41
Thomas Cushing	1

1786.	No. of Votes.
JAMES BOWDOIN	22
Benjamin Lincoln	8
Thomas Cushing	4

1787.	
JOHN HANCOCK	53
James Bowdoin	9
Benjamin Lincoln	7

1788.	
JOHN HANCOCK	68
James Bowdoin	4

1789.	
JOHN HANCOCK	59
James Bowdoin	1
Benjamin Lincoln	4

1790.	
JOHN HANCOCK	41
James Bowdoin	2

1791.	
JOHN HANCOCK	40
Caleb Strong	6
Benjamin Lincoln	4
Scattering	3

* No choice by the people; JAMES BOWDOIN elected by the Legislature.

1792.*	No. of Votes.
Francis Dana	27
Samuel Holton	27
Scattering	5

1793.	
JOHN HANCOCK	48
Samuel Phillips	3

1794.	
SAMUEL ADAMS	36
William Cushing	15
Scattering	9

1795.	
SAMUEL ADAMS	53
Moses Gill	9
Scattering	1

1796.†	
Increase Sumner	83
Edward H. Robbins	3
Moses Gill	1

1797.	
INCREASE SUMNER	96
Scattering	2

1798.	
INCREASE SUMNER	68
Scattering	1

1799.	
INCREASE SUMNER ‡	81

1800.	
CALEB STRONG	3
Elbridge Gerry	76
Scattering	4

1801.	
CALEB STRONG	51
Elbridge Gerry	34
Scattering	1

1802.	No. of Votes.
CALEB STRONG	82
Elbridge Gerry	28

1803.	
CALEB STRONG	83
Elbridge Gerry	10

1804.	
CALEB STRONG	80
James Sullivan	40

1805.	
CALEB STRONG	102
James Sullivan	67
Scattering	1

1806.	
CALEB STRONG	95
James Sullivan	67

1807.	
CALEB STRONG	118
James Sullivan	72

1808.	
Christopher Gore	105
JAMES SULLIVAN	74

1809.	
CHRISTOPHER GORE	121
Levi Lincoln	71
Scattering	2

1810.	
Christopher Gore	115
ELBRIDGE GERRY	73

1811.	
Christopher Gore	105
ELBRIDGE GERRY	64
Scattering	1

* Although Gov. HANCOCK was re-elected Governor in 1792, and by a great majority, yet he had not a single vote in Templeton.

† Although Gov. SAMUEL ADAMS was re-elected Governor in 1796, he had no votes in Templeton.

‡ No votes in Templeton for any one else.

1812.	No. of Votes.
CALEB STRONG	131
Elbridge Gerry	71
1813.	
CALEB STRONG	139
Joseph B. Varnum	54
1814.	
CALEB STRONG	139
Samuel Dexter	66
1815.	
CALEB STRONG	143
Samuel Dexter	66
1816.	
JOHN BROOKS	140
Samuel Dexter	74
1817.	
JOHN BROOKS	130
Henry Dearborn	62
1818.	
JOHN BROOKS	126
B. W. Crowningshield	54
1819.	
JOHN BROOKS	131
B. W. Crowningshield	68
1820.	
JOHN BROOKS	127
William Eustis	64
1821.	
JOHN BROOKS	108
William Eustis	63
1822.	
John Brooks	128
WILLIAM EUSTIS	65

1823.	No. of Votes.
Harrison Gray Otis	142
WILLIAM EUSTIS	91
Scattering	1
1824.	
Samuel Lathrop	160
WILLIAM EUSTIS	94
1825.	
Solomon Strong	13
LEVI LINCOLN	131
Scattering	1
1826.	
Samuel Hubbard	122
LEVI LINCOLN	74
James Lloyd	15
1827.	
LEVI LINCOLN	127
Scattering	13
1828.	
LEVI LINCOLN	119
Scattering	3
1829.	
LEVI LINCOLN	89
Marcus Morton	34
Samuel C. Allen	26
Scattering	1
1830.	
LEVI LINCOLN	161
Marcus Morton	10
Samuel C. Allen	16
1831.*	
LEVI LINCOLN	130
Scattering	7

* Since 1830, the political year in Massachusetts has commenced in January instead of May. Consequently, the governors voted for in November of each year, subsequent to 1830, did not assume their office till January of the following year.

1832.	No. of Votes.
LEVI LINCOLN	205
Marcus Morton	13
Samuel Lathrop (Antimasonic)	25

1833.	
John Davis *	200
Marcus Morton	19
John Quincy Adams (Antimasonic)	27
Scattering	1

1834.	
JOHN DAVIS	259
Marcus Morton	14
John Bailey (Antimasonic)	6

1835.	
EDWARD EVERETT	202
Marcus Morton	28

1836.	
EDWARD EVERETT	201
Marcus Morton	32

1837.	
EDWARD EVERETT	210
Marcus Morton	37

1838.	
EDWARD EVERETT	210
Marcus Morton	87

1839.	
Edward Everett	150
MARCUS MORTON	187

1840.	
JOHN DAVIS	224
Marcus Morton	160

1841.	No. of Votes.
JOHN DAVIS	194
Marcus Morton	142
Lucius Boltwood (Antislavery)	8

1842.	
John Davis	204
Marcus Morton †	142
Samuel E. Sewell (Antislavery)	7

1843.	
George N. Briggs ‡	167
Marcus Morton	142
Samuel E. Sewell	33

1844.	
GEORGE N. BRIGGS	172
George Bancroft	150
Samuel E. Sewell	38

1845.	
George N. Briggs §	149
Isaac Davis	126
Samuel E. Sewell	37
Henry Shaw	1

1846.	
GEORGE N. BRIGGS	178
Isaac Davis	120
Samuel E. Sewell	46
Francis Baylies	1

1847.	
GEORGE N. BRIGGS	151
Caleb Cushing	111
Samuel E. Sewell	39
Francis Baylies	3
Scattering	1

---

* JOHN DAVIS was elected by the Legislature, there being no choice by the people.

† No choice by the people; MARCUS MORTON elected by the Legislature.

‡ No choice by the people; GEORGE N. BRIGGS chosen by the Legislature.

§ No choice by the people; Gov. BRIGGS re-elected by the Legislature.

1848.	No. of Votes.
George N. Briggs *	140
Caleb Cushing	77
Stephen C. Phillips (Free Soil)	154
Scattering	1
1849.	
George N. Briggs *	132
George S. Boutwell	76
Stephen C. Phillips	129
1850.	
George N. Briggs	139
George S. Boutwell †	96
Stephen C. Phillips	133
1851.	
Robert C. Winthrop	168
George S. Boutwell ‡	85
John G. Palfrey	132
1852.	
John H. Clifford §	138
Henry W. Bishop	91
Horace Mann	153

1853.	No. of Votes.
Emory Washburn ‖	137
Henry W. Bishop	87
Henry Wilson	141
1854.	
Emory Washburn	62
Henry W. Bishop	26
Henry Wilson	14
HENRY J. GARDNER (American)	264
1855.	
Samuel H. Walley	31
Erasmus D. Beach	101
HENRY J. GARDNER	252
Julius Rockwell (Republican)	91
Scattering	1
1856.	
Luther V. Bell	5
Erasmus D. Beach	100
HENRY J. GARDNER	223
George W. Gordon	31
Scattering	19

SCHOOLS AND SCHOOLHOUSES.

There were no schools here before the incorporation of the town in 1762; at least, there were none supported by grants of public money. In 1763, there was a grant for a school. In 1764, the town was divided into "two squad-

---

* No choice by the people; Gov. BRIGGS re-elected by the Legislature.
† No choice by the people; GEORGE S. BOUTWELL chosen by the Legislature.
‡ No choice by the people; Gov. BOUTWELL re-elected by the Legislature.
§ No choice by the people; JOHN H. CLIFFORD elected by the Legislature.
‖ No choice by the people; EMORY WASHBURN elected by the Legislature.

rons" for schooling, — one on the westerly side, the other on the easterly. In 1773, a Committee was appointed "to squadron out the west part of the town for schooling." They made five school-divisions. In 1777, it appears that there were ten school-divisions in the whole township, including Phillipston. In 1769, it was voted that each school-district, or "squadron," should have the same proportion of money they paid for schooling. In 1776, the school-money was divided according to the number of children in each division between the ages of four and sixteen. This rule continued till 1779, when it was changed so as to divide according to the number between four and twenty-one years of age. This rule continued without change for almost fifty years. In 1822, and afterwards in 1827, some further allowance of money was made in favor of the smallest districts. In 1835, the method was adopted of dividing half of the school-money equally to each school, and the other half in proportion to the number of children. In 1805, the town voted to use the word "district" in all school-matters instead of "class," which had for some time previous been used.

No schoolhouses were built at public charge for many years. Schools were often kept in private houses. Then, in some of the districts, perhaps in all, schoolhouses were built by the voluntary contributions of the neighborhood. The first appropriation of *public money* for this purpose seems to have been in 1787. In that year, the town voted to take all the schoolhouses into its own charge, and to purchase of those who owned them what houses and frames were then existing in the several districts, at appraised values. All the schoolhouses in town amounted, however, to only £51: namely, No. 1 was valued at £15; No. 2, with all the materials provided for repairs, at £20; No. 3, at £4; No. 4, at £12. Nos. 5 and 6 had no houses to dispose of. The town then granted £120 (equal to $400) to build and repair schoolhouses throughout the town. A

Committee of the town determined their location. The same year, seven school "classes," or districts, were formed. In 1801, the rule was adopted for the town to allow each district, which might build a schoolhouse, a hundred dollars towards the cost, and the town to own and repair the houses; but, since 1814, they have been owned and repaired wholly by the districts. District No. 8 was formed, in 1831, by the division of No. 6; and District No. 9, in 1834, by the division of No. 3. The present District No. 1, at one time, formed two districts; namely, from 1815 to 1822. The present districts were legally defined by geographical lines in 1846.

During the first sixty-five years, the *legal* superintendence of the schools was vested in the Selectmen; but, in fact, the oversight of them was devolved mainly upon the minister. In 1811, the town, at the request of Rev. Mr. Wellington, chose a Committee to assist him in examining school-teachers. John W. Stiles and Josiah Howe were chosen. In 1815, the town chose a Committee of one from each district to assist in examining the schools, "and to recommend certain useful classical books." Committees "to regulate the school-books" and "examine the schools" were chosen afterward, at times, till the law for choosing School Committees went into operation. Still, up to that time, the care rested almost wholly upon the minister.

COMPARISON OF STATISTICS OF THE SCHOOLS.

The following tables show a comparison between the schools fifty years ago and at the present time, as to length and cost of schools, and the number of persons between the ages of four and twenty-one in each district: —

SUMMER SCHOOLS. — WAGES OF FEMALE TEACHERS.

Number of the District.	NAMES OF TEACHERS.	Year 1805–6.					1855–6.		
		Number between the Ages of 4 and 21 in 1805.	Length of School in Weeks.	Wages per Week.	Cost of Board per Week.	Total Cost of Wages and Board per Month.	Number between the Ages of 4 and 21 in 1855.	Length of School in Weeks.	Teachers' Wages per Month, including Board.
I.	Miss Millicent Kendall	96	12	$1.17	$0.92	$8.33	171	10	$20.50
II.	Miss Sally Fletcher . .	86	16	1.17	0.92	8.33	58	13	17.00
III.	Miss Betsey Sawyer . .	67	8	—	—	6.67	42	10	15.00
IV.	Miss Lydia Kendall . .	80	12	1.17	0.92	8.33	43	10	18.66
V.	Miss Silence Richardson	57	10	1.00	0.67	6.67	45	10	14.00
VI.	Miss Betsey Sawyer . .	53	8	1.17	0.92	8.33	144	18	20.00
VII.	Miss Patience Sawyer .	55	12	1.15	0.67	7.28	97	16	21.00
VIII.	(District formed in 1831) .	—	—	—	—	—	156	11	27.00
IX.	(District formed in 1834) .	—	—	—	—	—	121	10	20.00

WINTER SCHOOLS. — WAGES OF MALE TEACHERS.

Number of the District.	NAMES OF TEACHERS.	Year 1805–6.				1855–6.	
		Length of School in Weeks.	Teachers' Wages per Week.	Cost of Board per Week.	Male Teachers' Wages, including Board, per Month.	Length of School in Weeks.	Male Teachers' Wages per Month, including Board.
I.	Noah Kendall 2d	12	—	—	$22.67	(10)	$41.00
II.	Francis Fletcher	12	$4.00	$1.25	21.00	11	31.50
III.	Reuben Jones	8	3.25	1.58	19.33	7	29.00
IV.	Leonard Stone	8	3.50	1.33	19.33	14	*
V.	Reuben Jones	6	3.00	1.00	16.00	8	38.00
VI.	Leonard Stone	8	3.50	1.17	18.67	11	40.00
VII.	Artemas Baker	9	3.75	1.25	20.00	12	*
VIII.	(District formed in 1831) . .	—	—	—	—	9	*
IX.	(District formed in 1834) . .	—	—	—	—	12	40.00

* Female teacher.

From the foregoing figures, it appears, that, fifty years ago, the whole number of persons in town, between four and twenty-one years of age, was 494; while, in 1855, the number was 877. There were then seven districts and seven schools; there are now nine districts and twelve separate schools. The average length of the schools in the year 1805–6 was, in summer, eleven weeks; in winter, nine weeks. In 1855–6, the average length of the summer schools was twelve weeks; of the winter schools, ten and a half weeks. The average wages, including board, of the teachers of the summer schools, in 1805, was $1.94 a week; in 1855, it was $4.84 a week. The average wages of the male teachers in 1805–6, including board, was very nearly $20 a month; in 1855–6, the average was $36.75 a month. Reckoning both male and female teachers, therefore, the price of their services per month has a little more than doubled within the fifty years. Considering that the number of separate schools in the districts has increased from seven to twelve, and the number of children in the town in a still greater proportion (viz., from 494 to 877); and considering, also, that, fifty years ago, there was hardly any expense to the town for fuel (it being then customary for the people to provide it gratuitously), — it follows, that it now requires a town-grant of nearly $400 to provide schools for the town of the same length that $100 would have provided half a century ago.

It is now impossible to obtain any thing like a complete list of the school-teachers employed in this town in the successive years, or their wages. The following tables, however, will indicate, in some measure, the gradual advance in wages and board: —

FEMALE TEACHERS.

Years.

1770. Mrs. Job Whitcomb was paid for teaching four weeks, including her board, 20s. 6d., — equal to 86 cents a week.

Years.

1771. Paid for a teacher's wages, 3s. a week; for a teacher's board, 2s. 8d. a week.

1772. A teacher, not named in the records, was paid, for teaching twelve weeks, 2s. 8d. per week; her board cost 2s. 6d. per week, — equal to 86 cents a week, board and all.

1777. Silas Stone was paid £1. 16s. "for his wife's keeping school six weeks, and boarding her," — equal to $1 a week.

1792. Anna Taylor had 3s. 8d. a week for teaching.

In 1770, Dr. Benjamin Shattuck was paid, "for boarding a school-dame," at the rate of 2s. 8d. (44 cents) a week; and I find no instance, for twenty-five years after this, of more than 50 cents a week being paid for a female teacher's board.

MALE TEACHERS.

1770. Dr. Benjamin Shattuck was paid, for teaching school two and a half months, £6. 1s. 8d., — equal to $8.11 a month. Probably this included his board. The common price then for board of a master was 4s. 8d. (78 cents) a week. Joel Grout, however, had but 4s. a week in 1770.

1771. Paul Whitney's wages, for teaching four weeks, was 30s., — equal to $1.25 a week.

1773. Nathaniel Dickinson, "for keeping the town-school" five months, received £10.

1774. Josiah Grout, "for keeping school six weeks," had 6s. a week.

1776. Rev. Mr. Sparhawk boarded the schoolmaster at 5s. 6d. a week. I find no instance, before 1795, of more than $1 a week being paid for a male teacher's board. Of course, this remark, as well as that concerning female teachers' board not exceeding 50 cents a week, is with the exception of the *nominal* prices adopted between 1777 and 1780, while the continental paper-currency was depreciated.

1788. Aaron Hall's wages were £2. 5s. a month.

1789. Peter Holt's wages were £2. 14s. a month.

1792. Josiah Howe was paid $22 for teaching eleven weeks; and his board cost $1 a week more.

The following persons were paid as teachers in District No. 1, between the years 1794 and 1826, at the respective dates, prices, &c., named. The male and female teachers in the same line were employed the same year: —

Years.	MALE TEACHERS. Names of Teachers.	Length of School in Weeks.	Wages per Week, beside Board.	Cost of Board per Week.	FEMALE TEACHERS. Names of Teachers.	Length of School in Weeks.	Wages per Week, beside Board.	Cost of Board per Week.
1794	T. G. Fessenden. . . .	20	$2.50	$1.00	Hannah Cook	8	$0.83	$0.83
1800	Artemas Cook	6	4.00	1.17	Sally Parker	8	1.00	0.92
1803	George C. Shattuck *	10	3.50	1.00	Abigail Locke	8	1.58†	—
1805	Abraham Wheeler . .	6	4.00	1.42	Millicent Kendall . .	12	1.17	0.92
1810	Stephen Emory	6	4.50	1.33	Polly Cutting	12	2.25†	—
1815	Dr. David Goodridge .	12	6.00†	—	Achsah Richardson .	9	1.50	1.33
1820	Paul R. Kendall . . .	12	5.00	1.50	Lucy Wright	12	2.67†	—
1825	Thomas Sawyer	9	4.00	1.50	Lucy B. Howe	12	2.50†	—

The following persons were paid for teaching in District No. 2, between the years 1794 and 1827, at the respective dates, prices, &c., named:—

Years.	MALE TEACHERS. Names of Teachers.	Length of School in Weeks.	Wages per Week, beside Board.	Cost of Board per Week.	FEMALE TEACHERS. Names of Teachers.	Length of School in Weeks.	Wages per Week, beside Board.	Cost of Board per Week.
1794	Samuel Henry	8	$1.87½	$1.00	Abigail Sparhawk . .	8	$0.67	$0.50
1800	Moses Wright	8	3.50†	—	Anna Knowlton. . . .	8	1.00	0.67
1805	Abner Gay.	10	3.75	1.25	Sally Fletcher	16	1.17	0.83
1811	Oliver Fletcher . . .	12	4.00†	—	Beulah Goodridge . .	12	1.17	0.83
1815	. . . .	10	4.50	1.56	Charlotte Newton . .	10	2.33†	—
1820	David Spaulding . . .	9	4.50	1.56	Betsey Davis	10	1.92†	—
1825	Charles Osgood	10	3.75	1.17	Mary Ann Spooner . .	16	1.50	0.75
1827	Peter Cobleigh	11	4.00	1.10	. . . .	—	—	—

* The donor of the Athenæum shares hereinafter mentioned. † Including board.

SCHOOL-LAND AND MINISTERIAL LAND.

The original grant of the township by the Legislature required that three lots, each to be equal in value to the lot of one proprietor, should be set apart, and devoted, one to the first minister as his private property, which was of the nature of "a settlement;" one, the income or interest to be applied towards supporting the minister and his successors; and one, the income or interest to go towards supporting schools. These three "public lots" were accordingly set apart; viz., No. 46, No. 92, and No. 36. The first, of course, became the property of the Rev. Daniel Pond. No action was taken as to selling the other two lots till 1768, when it was at first voted to *lease* them both for nine hundred and ninety-nine years. But this was not carried into effect. It was decided to sell the school-land only at that time. Many years afterwards, — viz., in 1805, and again in 1810, — when the avails of the school-lands had disappeared, it was voted to petition the Legislature for leave to sell the ministerial lands, and apply the interest for schooling. But such a course was unlawful; and the plan of a school-fund was abandoned.

The school-lot was sold at auction, by vote of the town, May 15, 1769, to Deacon Phinehas Byam, for £55. 18s., — equal to $186.33. In 1770, it was also voted to apply the money from the sale of "pew-ground" in the meeting-house for four pews, as a perpetual fund for a school. In the pinching times of the Revolutionary War, which soon came on, it probably was not easy to keep funds on hand in the treasury; and the town perhaps thought, that, by granting school-taxes each year, they fulfilled sufficiently the intention of the Legislature. In 1788, a Committee recommended to the town that the interest on any notes remaining in the Treasurer's hands, after paying the town's debts, should be applied annually for the support of schools. But there is no further trace of any school-fund from such sources.

In 1837, however, when the town received its proportion of the surplus-revenue that had been distributed by the United States, amounting to $3,337.74 for this town, it was voted to loan that fund, and apply the interest for the support of schools. The interest was thus appropriated about three years; but in 1840, the town being in debt, the greater part of the fund was taken to pay the liability of the town in a suit in which Peter Sanderson recovered a large judgment against the town for damages sustained on the highway. Subsequently, what remained of the Surplus-revenue Fund was used in paying the town's debts.

The ministerial lot remained unsold for forty-four years after the sale of the school-lot. It consisted of two hundred and forty acres; the proprietors having exchanged some of the better lands belonging to it in the early divisions, and allowed a larger than the average quantity to this lot. The land was finally sold at auction, in eight parcels, July 6, 1813; and the committee took notes, payable to the trustees of the Ministerial Fund, for $1,312.97. The school-lot was sold, as above stated, in 1769, for £55. 18s. If that sum had been kept at compound interest, at five per cent, till the time of the sale of the ministerial land, it would have amounted to $1,594.45.

RESOLVES IN BEHALF OF AMERICAN FREEDOM.

The earliest action taken by the town, in its corporate capacity, in reference to the infringements on American liberties by the British government, was at a meeting held Dec. 31, 1772. The article in the warrant relating to this subject, and the proceedings upon it, are here copied from the Town Records. As a specimen of the style of the times, the extract conforms to the original spelling, capital letters, &c. The Article was in the following words: —

To lay before the Town the Proceedings of the Town of Boston with regard to our Charter Rights and libertyes, and to see if the Town will Communicate there Sentiments to the Town of Boston, Whether thay have Stated our Rights and the Infringements on them in a Propper light: — or act anything thereon as thay shall think Proper.

The record proceeds as follows: —

At a Very full Meeting of the freeholders and other Inhabitants of the Town of Templeton, Legally assembled on Thursday the 31 day of December Anno: Dom: 1772. Proceeded as follows, Viz. After Reading of a Pamphalet Containing a Statement of the Rights of the Colonists and of this Province in Perticular and the Infringements on those Rights, with the Letter of Corospondance from the Town of Boston — The Town then took those Important Matters Into their Serious Consideration — and it was put to Vote Whether the Town of Boston has stated our Charter Rights with the Infringements on them in a Propper Light — and it Pass[d] in the Affermative by a Very grate Majority, not one Dissenter — Then Voted to Choose a committee of Nine to Examin More Critically Into the Proceedings of the Town of Boston and to write an answer to their Letter of Corospondance and the Committee to Make Report at the adjournment of this Meeting.

At the adjourned meeting on the second Monday of January, 1773, this Committee made the following report, which is here given, together with a draught of a letter written by them to the Committee of Correspondence in Boston: —

Agreeable to the trust Reposed in us we have Taken Into further Consideration the Late Proceedings of the Town of Boston in Behalf of our Dieing libertyes — and we have carefully Perrused the grate and good Charter of the Province by which our liberties and Properties are Confirmed to us — And Therefore, we are fully of the opinion that the Town of Boston has Stated our Charter Rights and liberties, & the Infringements on them in a Very Convincing light to all Who are friends to our Happy and Glorious Constitution! And if these be the Dreary Circumstances We are in, In the Name of Reason, Where is our Inglish liberties for Which our Ancestors left their Goodly Habitations and Pleasant Gardens and Came to this then Howling Wilderness and Suffer[d] Hungar and Nakedness and almost every other Hardship? Was it that their Posterity should only for a few years Injoy those liberties and Previliges which Cost them So Much Blood, and then to be mad no more of than Beasts of Burthen? No Surely — but to Purchas for themselves and for us, their Posterity a free Constitution and quiet Habitations; and that as long as Time Shall Indure — Therefore, we, the sons of those Heroes, are under the gratest obligations to exert ourselves to the Utmost to Preserve Inviolate those Rights which God and Nature and the Charter of this Province Hath given us — Therefore, be it Voted, as the Opinion of this Town, that we have for some years past been loaded with Burthens to grate for the Shoulders of any Inglish-man to Bare: — and now, if, in addition to our other grevances, there Must be this, viz. that the Judges of the Superior Court be made Independent of the grants of this Province for their Support, it must have a direct Tendency to overthro and Distroy our happy Civil Government. — Voted secondly, that we will Cultivate a Close and Strict Union with Boston, and other Towns in the Province, and will heartily join with them in Every Lawful Step and Prudent way for the Redress of their and our Greivances. — Voted thirdly, that as the general Court is once more Permitted to Convene (and at their ancient Seat too) we, his Majesty's Loyal Subjects, in Town Meeting legally assembled, Doe hereby with our United Voice Humbly Intreat the Hon[le] House of Representatives to Use their gratest Influence for a full Redress of all our greivances.

To the Gentleman of the Committee for Corospondance and others in the Town of Boston: — We, the committee apointed by the Town at their Last Meeting to write an answer to your obligeing Letter of the 20th of November last, Do, at this Time, with grate Pleasure, both for ourselves and the Inhabitants of this Town, Return you our Sincear and Hearty Thanks for the grate care and pains you have from time to time bin at for the Supporting and Defending of our Invaluable Rights and liberties — But Espetially at this time when their Seems But a step between us and Ruin. It is true that, we, the Inhabitants of this Town have ben Inured to Hardships But thank God we dont look upon ourselves as yet creatures at *Human* Mercy — Therefore, you May Depend upon us that we will Concur with you, and the other Towns in the Province, in takeing Every Legal Step in order to obtain a full Redress of all greivances. We are very Sorry that your so Reasonable Request to the Governor was answered in Such a Manner — tis no doubt the effect of Independancy. Finally, we hope you will Continue to have an Eagle Eye upon our Sacred rights and liberties and Espye danger tho Ever so Remote — and our hope and Sincere Desires are that your Names Will be had in Everlasting Remembrance.

from your Most Humble and oblig[d] Servants —

JOHN RICHARDSON
JONATHAN BALDWIN
THOMAS WHITE
HENRY SAWTELL
JONAS WILDER
EBENEZER WRIGHT
SILAS JONES
ABEL HUNT
JOSHUA WRIGHT

The following resolves respecting goods imported from Great Britain were reported to the town, at a meeting held May 17, 1774, by a Committee chosen for the purpose, consisting of Abel Hunt, John Richardson, Jacob Grout, Thomas White, and Moses Gray. They were adopted by vote of the town: —

Voted, first, that we will not, by ourselves or by any under us, directly or indirectly, purchase any goods, of any person whatever, that is or shall be subject to any duty for the purpose of raising a revenue in America. Voted, second, that we will not use any foreign tea, nor countenance the use of it in our families, unless in case of sickness, and not then without a certificate from under the hand of one or more physicians that it is absolutely necessary in order for the recovery of their patient. And whoever in this town shall presume to act contrary to the aforementioned votes shall be deemed an enemy to his country, and treated as such.

REVOLUTIONARY WAR.

This town acted with great spirit and self-sacrifice in behalf of the American cause during the war. A Committee of correspondence, inspection, and safety, was annually chosen as long as the contest lasted. One or more companies of minute-men were formed. The following vote was passed Oct. 4, 1774: —

Voted that Samuel Osgood, Thomas White, Capt. Aaron Jones, Job Whitcomb, and William Sprague, provide provisions for our soldiers, and carry the same to them, in case they should be called for to go out to battle.

March 15, 1775, the town chose a Committee to take care of the minute-men's farms and families, if they should be called into battle. The Selectmen were instructed to procure fire-arms and ammunition at the charge of the town. William Sprague and Abel Hunt were paid for two days' work at "running bullets for the use of the town."

The next town-meeting warrant, after the battle of Lexington, was issued, not "in his majesty's name," as all previous warrants had been, but simply "by order of the Selectmen." In 1777, the warrants were issued "in the name of the government and people of the State of Massachusetts Bay." The town, many times during the war, provided beef and other provisions, and clothing, for the army; paid bounties for soldiers to enlist; and appointed committees to see to their families while absent. The Town Records do not show how many soldiers entered the army from this place. Capt. Joel Fletcher and Capt. Jonathan Holman each commanded a company, in the camp before Boston, in the autumn of 1775. In the year 1778, there were fifteen men from Templeton serving in the American army.

PRICES IN THE CONTINENTAL PAPER-MONEY.

During a portion of the Revolutionary War, the continental paper-money being a lawful tender, but at the same time enormously depreciated, of course the prices of labor and of all merchandise were greatly enhanced. All trade was brought thereby into a confused state. The method was adopted of fixing a schedule of prices, sometimes by the several towns, and sometimes by conventions in the counties or for the State, with a general understanding that the people should conform to those prices.

In October, 1779, a Convention was held at Concord for the purpose of "stating prices." This town chose Mr. Thomas White as its delegate to that Convention, and gave him the instructions which follow, as containing their views in regard to some particular articles which were deemed out of proportion in the then existing scale of prices. The instructions were reported, at a town-meeting held Sept. 30, 1779, by a Committee chosen by the town for that purpose, and were adopted by vote: —

To Mr. Thomas White.

Sir, — Whereas this town have made choice of you to represent this town in the State Convention to be holden at Concord on the first Wednesday of October next, nowise doubting but that you will use your utmost endeavors that all the affairs that shall come before you as a member of that Convention may be done with due regard to the interest of the community of which this town is a part, yet, sir, suffer us to mention some things to you that may help you easily to recollect what the sentiments of your constituents are on the affairs you are agoing upon.

As first, it is the mind of this town that there are too great disproportions in the price of things as now stated by the last Convention; namely, salt and rum, we conceive, are too high in proportion to mutton, veal, and lamb, which this town are of opinion are too low: for, although four shillings a pound seems to make a sound, what is it? Why, it is cheaper than it was even when our currency was looked upon equal to silver. Therefore, sir, 'tis the mind of this town that the price of mutton and veal ought to be raised, or the price of salt and rum brought lower: not that this town are desirous to rule the price of things, but that there might be an equality in the price of all. You will therefore use your influence that there may be an equality in the price of every article that shall come under the consideration of the Convention, and that a price be set so as to abide without any sudden alteration, and by no means to give your consent to a monthly alteration; for, if that should be effected, it will have a tendency to overthrow the whole.

You will keep your eye upon those who are enemies to the cause you are engaged in or agoing upon, — of which sort those herds of forestallers and monopolizers are who infest the land, — and represent them to the Convention in the light they properly deserve, and endeavor that some measure may be come into to put a stop to their infection, that it spread no farther; and that you will endeavor that some salutary measures may be come into to create a better understanding between the mercantile and the landed interests, which seem at present too wide apart: for they are both embarked in one cause; and whilst one is pulling one way, and the other the contrary, the public cause might suffer.

The Convention, it seems, left it optional with the several towns themselves to "state the prices" of various articles and of labor. This was immediately done by this town. The doings, with the list of prices, are copied below. It will serve not only to show the great depreciation of the paper-money, but to indicate the *comparative estimate* of articles and of labor in Templeton in 1779.

At a town-meeting, Oct. 19, 1779, it was —

Voted to choose a Committee of seven men to state the prices of such articles as they think necessary, and make report to the town at the adjournment of this meeting. Chose Capt. Richardson, Deacon Phinehas Byam, Jonathan Stratton, Capt. Jonathan Holman, Lieut. Leonard Stone, Thaddeus Brown, and Mr. Joseph White, for that purpose. Voted to adjourn the meeting to Friday, the fifth day of November next, at one o'clock in the afternoon, then to meet again at this place.

Friday, the fifth day of November, they met according to adjournment, and the Committee chosen to state the prices of such articles as should appear to them necessary made a report of prices which they had stated, as follows: —

Laborers in husbandry, £2. 14s. per day in the best of the season; and, at all other times in the year, in the usual proportion.
Blacksmith's shoeing a horse all round, steeling toe and heel, £4. Plain shoeing, &c., in the usual proportion.
A narrow-axe, of the best quality, £6; and all other edge-tools and smithing in the usual proportion.
Men's best shoes, £6 per pair.
Weaving yard-wide tow-cloth, 5s. per yard.
Women's labor, £2 per week.
Spinning fourteen knots of linen yarn, 5s.
Women's tailoring, 12s. per day. Tailoring taken in, in the usual proportion.
Horse-keeping, 16s. per night by hay, and 8s. by grass.
Keeping a yoke of oxen, £1. 1s. per night by hay, and 10s. by grass.
A good, common dinner, 14s.; and all other victualling in the usual proportion.
Lodging, 4s. per night.
New-England flip or toddy, 15s. per mug or bowl.
Cider, 4s. per mug.
Oats, per mess, 6s.
Shirts, £4. 16s. apiece, made of good tow-cloth seven-eighths of a yard wide, three yards and a half in each shirt.
Good yarn-stockings, £3. 12s. per pair.
Pasturing a yoke of oxen, £2. 2s. per week; a cow, 14s.
Keeping a yoke of oxen by hay, £3 per week; a cow, £1.
Sawing pine-boards, £10 per thousand feet; and all other sawing in the usual proportion.
Carpenter's work, in the best of the season, £3 per day.
Mason's work, £3. 6s. per day.
Bricks, £15 per thousand.
Rye, £4. 16s. per bushel; Indian corn, £3. 12s. per bushel; wheat, £8 per bushel; Oats, £2 per bushel.

This report of prices the town voted to adopt as the standard by which they would buy and sell. Women's work was valued much less, in proportion to that of men, than it is now.

All the prices stated probably were just twenty times as much as those previously current when payable in silver. About a year afterwards, the depreciation of the paper-money had increased so much, that the town paid Joseph White, Nov. 16, 1780, six hundred pounds in continental bills for twenty Spanish milled-dollars, being at the rate of a hundred dollars in paper for one in silver.

SECOND PRECINCT IN TEMPLETON, AND INCORPORATION OF GERRY, NOW PHILLIPSTON.

In the original township of Templeton, the meeting-house was considerably east of the centre of the territory. It was, consequently, quite inconvenient for those on the westerly side. In the winter season, especially, they felt very sensibly their distance from the house of worship. The town sometimes voted that Rev. Mr. Sparhawk might preach a few Sundays, in the course of the winter season, at the west part of the town, closing the meeting-house for the purpose. But they were not always willing to grant this favor. Much discussion and controversy ensued. The people of the westerly part of the town, weary of the inconvenience, petitioned the General Court, in 1773, to be separated from the rest of the town as to parochial affairs, and be made a distinct precinct or parish. The General Court, in 1774, granted the petition. As to most of the ordinary town-business, they were still to act together. It was a long time before the new parish felt able to sustain religious institutions. A church was first formed in that territory in 1785; and the first minister, Rev. Ebenezer Tucker, was ordained there Nov. 5, 1788. In 1786, Oct. 20, the Second Precinct, with a territory taken from the south-easterly part of Athol, was incorporated as a town, by the name of Gerry. The inhabitants, afterwards finding themselves decidedly opposed in political sentiment to Gov. Gerry, obtained an act to change the name to Phillipston.

In 1785, the town of Gardner was incorporated, and a tract included in it of some twelve or fifteen hundred acres set off from Templeton.

The following is the petition presented to the General Court, in 1773, in favor of setting off the Second Precinct: —

To his Excellency Thomas Hutchinson, Esq., Captain-General and Commander-in-chief in and over the Province of the Massachusetts Bay, to the Honorable his Majesty's Council and House of Representatives in General Court assembled at Boston, January, 1773: —

The petition of sundry inhabitants, living in the westerly part of the town of Templeton and the south-easterly part of the town of Athol, humbly shows: That the town of Templeton is so situated, that one house for public worship will in no wise serve the whole; that the proprietors of said Templeton have built one meeting-house, and placed it at a very considerable distance from the Centre, and where it well accommodates the easterly part of said Templeton, but will in no wise accommodate the inhabitants in the west part; that the west part of said Templeton is now considerably filled with inhabitants, and consists of the first settlers in said Templeton, who do and have labored under great difficulties and inconveniences for many years past by reason of living at such a great distance from public worship, a great part of whom live five miles and upwards, and being well situated with a part of the south-easterly part of the town of Athol to make a precinct. We therefore earnestly pray your excellency and honors would take our distressed and difficult circumstances into your wise consideration, and grant us relief (according to your usual practices in such cases) by dividing the town of Templeton into two precincts by the following line; viz.: Beginning in the northerly line of Hubbardston, on Burnshirt River; thence running up the river till it comes to a maple-tree, the corner of Second-division Lot No. 47; thence running north thirty degrees west till it comes to New Brook, so called; thence down said brook to Royalston Line. And also that the south-east part of the town of Athol be annexed to Templeton, to accommodate said west part of Templeton, by the following line; viz.: To run north-easterly from the most westerly corner of Templeton to the west corner of Isaac Ball's land that he now dwells on; from thence north-easterly to Miller's River, where Thousand-acre Brook empties into said river; thence up said river to Royalston Line. Or grant relief to your petitioners in such other way and manner as your excellency and honors shall think most proper.

SAMUEL TAYLOR.	REUBEN CUMMINGS.
JOSEPH WHITE.	CHARLES BAKER.

[And forty-nine others.]

JANUARY the 7th, 1773.

The following action on the petition was taken by the General Court in 1774: —

In Council, Feb. 15, 1774: Read, and ordered that the tract of land hereafter described, lying partly in Templeton and partly in Athol, together with the inhabitants thereon dwelling, be, and hereby are, erected into a precinct; and the said inhabitants are hereby invested with all the powers and privileges by law belonging to inhabitants of precincts in this province: viz., beginning at Hubbardston Line where Burnshirt Stream runs out of Templeton; thence running up said stream to a maple-tree, being the southerly corner of the Second-division Lot No. 47; thence running north thirty degrees west to New Brook, so called; thence down the brook to Royalston Line; thence west to Athol Line, being the north-west corner of Templeton, then on Athol Line to Miller's River; thence down said river to a brook called Thousand-acre Meadow Brook; thence south-easterly to the westerly corner of the Hundred-acre Lot No. 22, then straight to the most westerly corner of Templeton; thence by Templeton Line to where it began. And further ordered, that Abner Sawyer, Abraham Sawyer, Joel Grout, Samuel Lamb, Joshua Whitcomb, John Brigham, —— Alexander, jun., —— Davis, Thomas ——, Jonathan Willington, Elias Sawyer, Calvin Reed, Ebenezer Knight, Isaac Ball, jun., Israel Sprague, Joseph Morse, Benjamin Parsons, John Colman, Robert Young, jun., and Zaccheus Rich, with their estates, together with the farm of Capt. Aaron Jones of a hundred and twenty-four acres adjoining the easterly line, although included within the precinct hereby erected, be, and hereby are, exempted from doing duty there, but shall be subject to do duty in the precinct in which they were respectively included before the passing of their order, unless they, or either of them, within nine months from the date hereof, return their names into the secretary's office, signifying their desire to belong to the said precinct; in which case they shall be considered as belonging to the said precinct, and shall do duty and receive privileges accordingly.

Sent down for concurrence. JONA. COTTON, *Dep. Sec.*

In the House of Representatives, Feb. 16, 1774: Read and concurred. J. CUSHING, *Speaker*.

Consented to. THOMAS HUTCHINSON [*Governor*].

No effectual movements were made for several years by the Westerly or Phillipston Precinct for sustaining religious institutions. In 1784, fourteen of the inhabitants, becoming tired of their situation, petitioned to be united again to the First Precinct. The following is a copy of the petition, and of the doings of the town thereon: —

To the Inhabitants of the First Precinct in Templeton: —

The petition of us, the subscribers, inhabitants of the West Parish in said Templeton, humbly showeth: That your petitioners having been for a number of years set off with said West Parish, but having had many unforeseen difficulties to encounter with, so that it has never been in our power to build a meeting-house, nor to furnish ourselves with but very little preaching; nor can we, by looking forward, see any better prospect, — your petitioners therefore pray that we may be re-united to your precinct again, upon these express conditions: viz., that we never move to have your meeting-house moved or rebuilt on any other spot than where it now stands; but in case our whole parish, or so many of them as live in Templeton, should be re-united to your precinct, then, in that case, we pray the town to grant them four days' preaching in each year, either by money for that purpose, or any other way that the precinct think best.

As your petitioners, in duty bound, shall ever pray, &c.

Thos. Johnson.	Thos. White.
David Knight.	Jona. Stratton.
John Hager, jun.	Simeon Hayward.
Hannah Sawyer.	William Dike.
Elisha Parker.	Benjamin Gallop.
Samuel Lamb.	Ruth White.
Joshua Wilder.	Edmund Brigham.

Templeton, Jan. 6, 1784.

The First Precinct voted to receive the petitioners agreeably to their petition. The record also says, —

Voted to receive the whole of said parish that belong to Templeton, if they are disposed to be re-united to us again, upon the conditions of the petition of Thomas White and others. Voted that the Committee serve the whole of said parish with a copy of these votes, intimating our desire that they may be re-united to us again.

PAUPERS.

This town has never been subjected to so great expense for the support of paupers as many other towns. In early times, a "settlement" — rendering the town liable for the individual's support in case he became a pauper — was acquired, in one mode, by a person's being received as an "inhabitant" of a town, in a technical sense. Hence arose the usage, in those days, of the Selectmen issuing a precept to the constable to "warn out" all new-comers. Not that they were actually expected or desired to leave the town; but the process prevented the town where the persons had their previous "settlement" from escaping its liability for their future support. At first, it was the practice here for the Selectmen thus to "warn out" all, without exception, who came to reside in the town; and whoever admitted any from another town into his family or into his tenement was required to give the Selectmen written notice, stating their names, former place of abode, and their circumstances in respect to property. In May, 1763, there was an article in the warrant "to see whether the town will still insist on the Selectmen's warning out all the persons that come into town." It "passed in the negative." Many persons were warned out during the next few years. The "warning-out laws" were repealed April 10, 1767. It is said, that, from that date till June 23, 1789, no pauper-settlement could be gained in a town merely by residence therein. The following specimens of the notices concerning new-comers arriving, and of notices to warn them out, are copied from the early records. Initials are substituted, in most cases, for the full names which appear on the records: —

To the Selectmen of Templeton.

Gentlemen, — I have taken in to live with me Jacob Puffer, who came from Sudbury, and, by what I can learn, a man of good estate; and he came to this town April the 11th; and I have taken him into my house to reside. Yours, &c., Abel Hunt.

May 11, 1764.

To the Selectmen of Templeton.

GENTLEMEN, — I have taken into my house, the twenty-second or the twenty-third day of November, James B——, and Mary or Molly his wife, and Betty their child, who came from Marlborough; and, whether rich or not, I can't tell.

From your humble servant, JOHN RICHARDSON.

NOV. 28, 1764.

To the Selectmen of Templeton.

GENTLEMEN, — This may inform you that I have taken in, to dwell in my house, William B——, and Sarah his wife. The said William was born in Littleton, but came last from Stow. Said Sarah was born in Acton, and came directly from that place, and is daughter of Capt. Daniel F——, of said Acton; their circumstances being small, they just beginning to set up house-keeping. And also I have taken into my house, as an hired maid, one Abigail F——, daughter of Benjamin F——, of Concord: she came directly from her father's house. I received all the above-named persons into my house this day, being June the 7th, 1769.

Yours, &c., CHARLES BAKER.

The following is a copy of one of the warrants used, in 1765, for "warning out" residents. The original spelling and grammar are preserved: —

WORCESTER, *ss.* Templeton Aprel ye 25 — 1765. — To Abraham Sawyer one of the Constables of Templeton; Greeting — you are Required in his majisties Name forthwith to Warn out the Persons here after mentioned, James B—— and his Wife Mary and Molley their Daughter Last from Marlborough — the Selectmen of the town Refuse to accept you for Inhabitants in S[d] Town, and you are not to abide any longer — and you are forthwith to make Return of this Warrent With your Doings unto Sum one of the Selectmen.

JASON WHITNEY,
JOSHUA CHURCH,
SAMUEL SAWYER,
JONATHAN HOLMAN, } *Selectmen of Templeton.*

WORCESTER, *ss.* May 9. — By Virtue of this Warrent I have Done as Within ordered.

ABRAHAM SAWYER,
Constable.

For the first forty or fifty years after the incorporation of the town, the expenses for the support of the poor were very moderate. The records indicate that they were kindly treated, and that cases demanding relief were met in a good spirit. In 1764, the town voted to hire for a year, of Mr. Joshua Church, "his old house for a work-house" (probably built of logs), and to pay him thirteen shillings and fourpence rent. In 1777, the town voted to build a house on the Common for the paupers, one story high, eighteen feet by thirty-six; but I find no traces, in the Treasurer's books or elsewhere, of this house having ever been actually built.

At that period, the paupers were usually supplied at their own abodes with so much as was necessary, or were boarded out by the Selectmen, often among their friends. In 1796, it was voted that the support of the poor should be let out at auction, with the express provision "that they be civilly and kindly treated." In 1815, the Selectmen were directed to let out the supporting of the poor that year by private contract. In 1817, the town voted not to build a poor-house; and they were let out, "in lots," "to the lowest bidder:" the overseers, however, to bind out such minors as were of suitable age. In 1818, they were let out at auction, apparently all together. During many years, the method of their support was left to the discretion of the Selectmen. Thirty years ago, the subject of providing an alms-house for their permanent abode was discussed. A Committee of the town reported then, that a poor-house for this town would increase the expense; and recommended the town to unite, if practicable, with Phillipston, Athol, Royalston, and Winchendon, to purchase one large farm, and erect buildings for all the poor of those towns. But, in 1827, the town agreed to purchase the farm that was owned by Moses Wright, Esq., then lately deceased, and to occupy it for the abode and support of the poor. The plan worked favorably. The establishment was superintended, for the first nine years, by Mr. Roper; and the Selectmen reported that it had given great satisfaction, and been well managed. In 1837, the Selectmen were authorized to build an addition to the house. In 1844, the pine-timber on the farm was sold for about three thousand dollars. During the last twenty years, it has been superintended by several persons in succession; and the inmates are, and have constantly been, made thoroughly comfortable, and amply provided for, at a very moderate expense to the town. The number of paupers is now smaller than for many years previous. According to the last report of the Selectmen, the whole number whose support is at the cost of the town, both in and out of the poor-house, is only five.

PETITION TO THE SELECTMEN.

The following petition serves to illustrate the feeling of the first generation of settlers here respecting habits of intemperance and dissipation, and the methods to which they resorted to check it. It is copied *verbatim* from the original: —

To the Selectmen of the Town of Templeton.

GENTLEMEN, — We the subscribers Humbly Show that Mr. —— was out from home about three weeks in the fore part of the Last winter, a spending his time and money by Drinking and Tippling, from house to house and Town to Town — and now he has took another voyage on the same arrand and has bin gone from home a month or More, and his family a suffering at home — We pray you forthwith, to take speedy Care of him by Posting him as the Law directs, or by Taking some good Custom to prevent him from spending his Estate so that his Family may have a comfortable support and not to become a Town Charge — And in so doing you will Much oblig, Yours &c. &c.

[Signed by thirty persons.]

TEMPLETON, March 23, 1778.

"WOLF ACT." — BOUNTIES FOR CROWS AND HAWKS.

April 7, 1783, the town voted to give a bounty of forty shillings for each grown wolf's head, and chose a Committee, who reported the following rules, which were adopted: —

Enacted that any person, who is an inhabitant of the town of Templeton, shall receive forty shillings out of the treasury of said Templeton for each wolf he or they shall kill within fifty miles of this place; and, in order to entitle any persons to the aforesaid bounty, he or they shall produce the skin into the presence of the Selectmen of the town, whose duty it shall be to cut the ears off of said skin, and give the said person that killed the wolf an order on the Town Treasurer for the aforesaid forty shillings: provided always, that the person so presenting a skin as aforesaid shall take his oath (if required) that he killed the wolf within the limits aforesaid, and that he was killed after the 7th of this instant (April, 1783). Be it further enacted, that every person shall receive twenty shillings, in the manner aforesaid, for each wolf's pup; the Selectmen to be judges which are pups, and which not. And, if any person is sworn, it shall be in the presence of the Selectmen. This Act to be in force one year, and no more.

This offer of bounty, or "Wolf Act," as the town called it, was renewed on the same conditions, for one year longer, in 1784, and so also in 1785 and 1786. Capt. Gardner Maynard was paid forty shillings for a wolf killed by him in 1783. Bears were occasionally killed in the township in early times.

In 1797, the town offered a bounty of thirty-four cents for each old crow's head, and seventeen cents for young ones, if killed from April 1 to July 1. A bounty on crows was offered several other years: the last was in 1834. In 1801 and 1802, a bounty of twenty-five cents and twelve and a half cents was offered for the heads of old and young hen-hawks. The heads of the crows and hawks were to be carried to the Selectmen, and they were to order the pay.

WARNING TOWN-MEETINGS.

Town-meetings seem to have been, at first, warned by personal notice to each voter. For instance, the constable's return upon the warrant for the third town-meeting held here says, "In obedience to the above warrant, I have warned *all that I suppose to be* the votable inhabitants of said town to meet at the time and place above mentioned."

As early as 1764, the practice was adopted for the Selectmen to issue *two* warrants, duplicates, for each meeting,— one directed to the constable for the east side of the town, the other to the constable for the west side, each to warn their own part of the town. These duplicate warrants were *both* copied into the records, with the return upon them, as long as both parts of the town remained together. The earliest intimation that I find of warning meetings by posting copies of the warrants is in 1769, when the town voted, "that posting a copy of the warrant on a post erected for that purpose shall be a sufficient warning for the east side;" and, for the west side, it shall be sufficient "to post a copy at the house of Charles Baker:" to be done fourteen days before the time of meeting.

TOWN-HOUSES.

The town-meetings, from the first, were held in the old meeting-house, and as long as that stood. The town-officers frequently, or generally, met at Landlord Wright's tavern. In 1811, when the new meeting-house had been erected, it was voted to sell the old meeting-house, and apply the proceeds to build a town-house. A Committee was appointed with full powers to act at their discretion for procuring a town-house. One was built, using the timbers of the first meeting-house, and finished in the summer of

1812. It stood on the present site of Mrs. Newton's dwelling-house. In 1844, School District No. 1 being about to build a schoolhouse, the town united with the district, and erected the present brick building, under certain specified conditions as to the joint ownership and repairs by the town and district. The new Town Hall cost the town somewhat over two thousand dollars. In 1846, the town authorized the sale of the old Town House, with the land under and adjoining it.

PAYMENT OF ACCOUNTS AGAINST THE TOWN.

It was customary for more than forty years after the incorporation of the town, as it always had been at meetings of the proprietors, to have all accounts, presented by individuals against the town, laid before the town in detail, and accepted, each by special vote, before the Selectmen should pay them. The practice began to be changed in 1808. That year, the Selectmen were made a Committee to allow accounts, except their own (which were still to be laid before the town). A similar vote was passed in 1811 and in 1813, and afterwards annually for a number of years, till it became the settled practice, which continues to the present time, to leave it to the Selectmen, in all ordinary cases, to adjust and make payment of claims against the town.

TREATY WITH GREAT BRITAIN.

At that critical period of American history, near the close of Washington's administration, when the question was before Congress as to carrying into effect the treaty with Great Britain negotiated by John Jay, with the discussion of which the eloquence of Fisher Ames will always be associated, the town of Boston sent a circular letter to the interior towns, containing the draft of a memorial to Congress in favor of the treaty, and recommending the towns to adopt it. The occasion was justly viewed as a very important one. Rev. Mr. Sparhawk, on Sunday, May 8, 1796, requested the male inhabitants of Templeton to assemble the next day to express their minds on the subject. The meeting voted to adopt "the memorial from Boston, and sign the same," and directed Col. Silas Hazeltine and Mr. Thomas Fisher to write the names of such as should personally request it. One hundred and eighty persons ordered their names to be set to the memorial; and it was "voted that the Selectmen, with the Moderator and Town Clerk, shall certify that every person whose name is set to it was present, and ordered it to be done; and also to certify that the inhabitants were perfectly united, and that there was not a single dissentient."

It may be considered as a further index of the spirit of the inhabitants, that at a special meeting for the purpose, on the 8th of July, 1794, when there were some apprehensions of war, the town voted that each soldier who should voluntarily enlist into the service of the United States, agreeably to the act of Congress of May 9, should have his pay made up by the town to forty shillings a month, "in case they shall be called into actual service, and that the government should not make up their pay to that amount within one year of the expiration of their enlistment."

SECOND WAR WITH ENGLAND.

A considerable number of persons from the militia of this town were called into service during the war of 1812–15, mostly for short periods, and to guard the forts in Boston

Harbor and on other parts of the New-England sea-coast. I have not found any records of the names of the men. During the embargo which preceded the war, the town voted, in 1808, to petition the President of the United States to suspend the embargo, in whole or in part, and appointed a Committee to draw up a memorial. In 1809, the town voted to petition the Legislature of the Commonwealth, praying them "to petition the Congress of the United States to relieve them from the embarrassments which they severely experience from the Embargo Law." The same year, the town voted "to provide, and keep constantly under the control of the Selectmen, powder, balls, and flints, for the use and benefit of the soldiers in this town."

When the war was declared, in 1812, the town voted to present a memorial to the President against the war, and for the restoration of peace. A Committee, consisting of Rev. Elisha Andrews, Rev. Charles Wellington, Lovell Walker, Esq., Samuel Cutting, Esq., John W. Stiles, Leonard Stone, and Deacon Paul Kendall, reported a very elaborate memorial, entering largely into argument upon the subject. It covers twelve pages in the Town Records, and was adopted by a vote of eighty-six to twenty-two. The memorial was the composition of Mr. Stiles, who was then a merchant in this town, — a man of great vigor and mental ability.

CANAL AND RAILROADS.

Great attention was always given in this town to improvement of roads; and the public-spirited citizens early perceived the importance of some more feasible modes of communication than the common highways or turnpikes. Before railroads had been introduced or thought practicable, a plan was started for a canal from Boston to the Hudson River. Surveys were made, both in the northern and southern portions of the State, to find a practicable route, especially by Loammi Baldwin, Esq., an engineer of high reputation. In 1825, this town chose a Committee, consisting of Col. Ephraim Stone, Col. Leonard Stone, Joshua Richardson, Esq., Col. Artemas Lee, and Capt. Eden Baldwin, with directions "to examine a route for a canal through Templeton, and to wait upon the Canal Commissioners when they pass through this part of the country."

But it was soon found that railroads are far better adapted to New England than canals; and, from the first, this town has acted with great vigor and earnestness to secure facilities of transport in this manner. Before the Fitchburg Railroad had been projected, the town, in 1835, raised money, and appointed a Committee to act in favor of a railroad from Worcester to Keene, N.H., through this town. In 1844, the town passed resolves in favor of the location of the Vermont and Massachusetts Railroad, and chose a Committee to act in its favor. After the road had been chartered, and its location determined to pass through Templeton, those who had control of the corporation undertook to alter it so as to pass through Winchendon, and leave this town at a distance from railroad facilities. This was strenuously opposed, both by individuals, who contributed largely of their time and money, and by the town in its corporate capacity, which appropriated funds and appointed committees to resist the change. Surveyors were employed, counsel retained, and long trials had, both before the County Commissioners of Worcester and before committees of the Legislature. The Committee to whom it was intrusted by the town consisted of Col. Artemas Lee, Capt. Joseph Davis, Joseph Mason, Esq., Gilman Day, Esq., and Col. Leonard Stone.

The County Commissioners, after a long hearing of evidence at Baldwinville in 1845, had decided against changing the location of the railroad from Templeton. The company, however, again petitioned the Legislature for leave to alter the location. In November, 1845, the town passed some very spirited resolves on the subject, setting forth the case in forcible language and at considerable length. In 1846, the Committee of the town were directed to oppose, before the Legislature, the petition of the railroad company, and to employ counsel. The final result was, that the General Court refused to change the location; and the road was built here. Passenger-cars passed through this town, for the first time, in 1847. The stock in the Vermont and Massachusetts Railroad has not been profitable; but the accommodation to the town and benefit to its business have been very great, and perhaps may, at a future time, become greater than now.

In 1847, the town authorized a Committee to advocate the petition of David Henshaw and others for a charter for a railroad from Worcester to Keene. Similar action was taken, in 1848 and 1851, in favor of contemplated routes for roads leading across the county to connect with the Boston and Worcester and the Western railroads. But these enterprises have not as yet been carried into effect.

COUNTY-RELATIONS.

The county of Worcester contains fifty-eight towns. Templeton stands at very nearly the average of the towns in the county, in respect to both population and valuation. At the time of the Revolutionary War, Templeton (then including most of Phillipston) paid about one dollar in sixty-six of the tax levied by the county. The portion of territory remaining to Templeton has increased, as to valuation, more rapidly than the average of the county: for the town now pays one dollar in sixty-three of the county-tax; and Phillipston pays, besides, one dollar in a hundred and fifty.

The project of separating the north part of Worcester County to form a new county, with the addition of other towns out of the county, lying either to the west or to the east, has been discussed, at various periods, for almost a hundred years. The idea was sometimes entertained, that, in the event of a new county, Templeton would be the shire-town. Petersham was sometimes proposed. A great many conventions have been held in this region, and town-action often taken on the subject, from the period of the Revolution till now. At one of the earliest town-meetings held after the incorporation of Templeton, — viz., Aug. 9, 1763, — Joshua Willard, Esq., was chosen an agent, in behalf of Templeton, to act "at the Great and General Court concerning a new county."

In 1781, the town acted upon a letter from the town of Warwick respecting a new county, and appointed a delegate to a convention at Petersham, but with instructions not to join in the petition, unless the towns of Westminster, Ashburnham, Fitchburg, Ashby, Lunenburg, and Leominster should be included. In 1784, Charles Baker was chosen an agent to act for a division of Worcester into two counties. But the opinions of the majority of the town varied; for, the next year, they refused to send a member to a convention on the subject at Petersham. Not long after, a Committee was chosen to act in the matter, but was dismissed in a few months. In 1791, the town, at first, sent delegates to a convention called at Petersham, concerning a new county; but, in August of the same year, "the town, by vote, signified their disapprobation of a new county." In 1792, an effort was made to unite, for county-purposes, nineteen towns; of which Ashburnham was the most easterly, and Pelham and Shutesbury the most westerly. But the town voted "that its agent should not sign said petition." In 1794, there was another similar refusal. In 1796, the plan of building a new court-house at Worcester was entertained. The people feared the expense, and remonstrated against it, assigning three general grounds: first, that the county of Worcester was too large, and, if divided, the existing court-house would be sufficient;

second, that, if not divided, the court-house ought to be nearer the centre; third, that it was a bad time to build, materials and labor being so high. The last difficulty, we may believe, has not been remedied during the whole sixty years from that day to this.

The town accordingly, for several years, favored a division. In 1798, they voted for it eighty-four to one. The efforts did not succeed, and the subject was dropped for a time. It was renewed in 1810, when a convention was called to meet in this town on the matter; and a petition on behalf of the town, for a division, was forwarded to the Legislature. But in 1828, on the question of a new county, according to the petition of Ivers Jewett and others, to be composed of sixteen towns in Worcester and five in Middlesex, the vote of the town was — yeas, four; nays, a hundred and twenty-six. During the efforts made from 1851 to 1855 in behalf of a new county, the town, though not with such unanimity as in 1828, constantly remonstrated against the measure, and repeatedly chose Col. Artemas Lee a Committee to join with Committees of other towns to oppose the project. These latter movements contemplated making Fitchburg the shire-town. The petitions were not granted by the Legislature. But at length, in 1856, Fitchburg was made a "half-shire" by establishing there two civil terms of the Court of Common Pleas for the county of Worcester each year, — viz., on the first Monday of February and the fourth Monday of October, — and one criminal term each year on the first Monday of June.

JEHU RICHARDSON FUND AND MASONIC FUND.

In 1827, the town voted to accept a charity-fund bequeathed by Jehu Richardson, of this town, for the benefit of unmarried females, of good character, in indigent circumstances. In 1843, the Masonic Lodge, when dissolved, gave its funds to the town, in trust, for the relief of the indigent, with stipulations as to the annual increase of the fund very similar to some made in Mr. Richardson's will. These provisions appear in the following report made to the town by the Committee of the Lodge: —

The undersigned, a Committee chosen by the members of Harris Lodge, resident in Templeton, to present to the town that portion of the funds of said lodge belonging to them, to be held by the town in trust, the income of which to be appropriated to charitable purposes, beg leave to report: —

That whereas the institution of Masonry was originally designed for laudable purposes and ends, — among which, as a cardinal virtue, was that of charity; and whereas the designs of this institution, like other human institutions, have been perverted, and its character thereby prejudiced, and in consequence thereof, and from the history of events, it has been deemed expedient by the members of the Harris Lodge, in obedience to public sentiment and the laws, to dissolve said lodge; and whereas, upon its dissolution, there was a fund which fell to the members of Templeton, amounting to four hundred dollars, — therefore, to the end that the objects and designs of the institution, and especially the aforesaid fund, shall not be perverted and misapplied, but that the integrity of the lodge should be kept, and the fund perpetuated by them, the members of the fraternity, by their Committee, propose to deposit said fund in the hands of the town, to be held in *trust*, and to be called the Masonic Fund, and upon the following conditions: —

That the town annually, at their March or April meeting, choose three Trustees, whose duty it shall be to see that the fund is safely invested upon good security on interest annually, payable to the Treasurer of the town; or, in the event the town should appropriate the fund to its own use, the town to give an obligation payable to the Trustees as aforesaid, and in such form as will designate the name of the fund. One per cent of this interest shall be annually added to the principal; and the residue of the income arising therefrom said Trustees shall pay out annually to such needy and destitute persons belonging to the town as they may think the most worthy and deserving of the same, with special regard to their merits; and the said Trustees shall report annually in writing, at the March or April meeting, their doings and the state of the fund, and before a new choice of Trustees is made.

EPHRAIM STONE,
LEONARD STONE,
ARTEMAS LEE, } *Committee of the Lodge.*

TEMPLETON, April 3, 1843.

The town annually elects Trustees of the Masonic Fund, and also of the Richardson Fund. The capital of both is, at present, loaned to the town, and interest paid annually, with addition of the one per cent to the principal. The amount of the Richardson Fund is a little over seven hundred dollars; of the Masonic, about four hundred and fifty dollars.

DONATION, BY DR. SHATTUCK, OF SHARES IN THE BOSTON ATHENÆUM.

In 1854, Dr. George C. Shattuck, of Boston, since deceased, gave five shares in the Boston Athenæum to the town of Templeton, in token of his affection for the place of his birth. These shares are to be perpetually held in trust for the following purposes, as expressed by the donor: "That the Selectmen of the town, for the time being, shall permit the use of the five shares, from year to year, by any one five persons resident in said town, to be selected by them from the classes of clergymen, physicians, lawyers, teachers, and scientific farmers and mechanics; it being understood that the said shares themselves are to be for ever inalienable." In addition to the cost of the shares (three hundred dollars each), Dr. Shattuck anticipated the annual assessment of five dollars a share by paying a hundred dollars in advance, additional, on each; thus securing the perpetual privilege of taking out books, on the shares, from the excellent library of the institution.

The town, on the reception of this donation, passed a vote of thanks to Dr. Shattuck, in acknowledgment of "their grateful appreciation of his munificence in conferring this franchise upon the town which has the honor of numbering him among her most distinguished and useful sons." A similar donation was made by him to the town of Littleton, the birthplace of his father.

Dr. Shattuck was an eminent physician in Boston, where he practised from 1807 till his death in 1854. He was graduated at Dartmouth College in 1803; was possessed of much wealth; and was distinguished for his benefactions to the needy. He gave liberally to Dartmouth College and to Harvard College, and to various public institutions, both in his lifetime and by his will.

A discourse has been printed, preached on the occasion of his death by Rev. Mr. Bartol, minister of the West Church in Boston, where Dr. Shattuck was a communicant. He was son of Dr. Benjamin Shattuck, who was born in Littleton, and was grandson of the first minister of that town. Dr. Benjamin Shattuck (H. U. 1765) studied medicine with Dr. Prescott, of Groton. He came to Templeton, by invitation of the people of the town, about 1769, and continued in active practice here till his death in 1794. He was a warm and intimate friend of Rev. Mr. Sparhawk, of whose church he was a member. A discourse preached at his funeral, by Mr. Sparhawk, was published at the time.

POPULATION.

The number of inhabitants in Templeton, at various periods, has been as follows:—

In 1765 (including the territory in Phillipston), it was	348
In 1790 (after the separation of Phillipston)	950
In 1801	1,068
In 1811	1,205
In 1821	1,331
In 1831	1,552
In 1840	1,776
In 1850	2,173
In 1855	2,618

VALUATION.

The successive State-valuations have been as follows. The first four were computed on a reduced scale of six per cent of the estimated value: —

1790	£1,944. 17s. 11d.
1801	$8,593.52
1811	10,444.93
1821	13,294.55
1831	378,358.00
1840	581,845.00
1850	877,725.00

In 1856, the Assessors' inventory of property taxable in this town was $1,026,283: namely, real estate, $592,676; personal estate, $433,607. The number of polls taxed was seven hundred and fifty.

MANUFACTURES AND PRODUCTIONS.

The Assessors of each town, in the year 1855, were directed to return to the Secretary of the Commonwealth the statistics of the various branches of industry for that year. The following are some of the most important items reported by the Assessors of Templeton: —

Cassimere. — 7 sets of machinery; 275,000 pounds of wool consumed; 220,000 yards of cloth manufactured; value, $198,000. Persons employed, — males, 85; females, 45.

Iron-castings. — 300 tons; value produced, $24,000; men employed, 15.

Machinery. — Value, $10,000; men employed, 10.

Tin-ware manufactured. — Value, $36,000.

Boots, 34,000 pairs; shoes, 1,700 pairs. — Value of boots and shoes, $46,000; number of men employed, 92.

Lumber prepared for market. — Value, $18,000.

Wooden-ware. — Value, $50,000; persons employed, 61.

Chair-seat frames. — Value, $5,000; persons employed, 10.
Chairs, including cabinet furniture. — Value, $164,900; males employed, 139; females employed, 150.
Carriages. — Value, $2,000.
Various other articles manufactured, included in the returns; to the value of about $67,000.

The quantity of land in the town occupied with the various kinds of grain, and statistics of other agricultural productions, were reported as follows: —

		Average produce per acre.
Indian corn	174 acres	35 bushels.
Wheat	14 "	16 "
Rye	20 "	10 "
Barley	106 "	25 "
Oats	87 "	30 "

Number of acres of potatoes (113 bushels to acre)	163
Number of acres of English mowing	2,239
Number of tons of English hay cut	1,690
Number of tons of meadow hay cut	529
Number of apple-trees cultivated for their fruit	4,313
Number of oxen over three years old	193
Number of steers under three years old	147
Number of milch cows	530
Number of heifers	198
Number of horses	327

THE END.

www.ingramcontent.com/pod-product-compliance
Lightning Source LLC
LaVergne TN
LVHW011230110826
845150LV00006B/1594
* 9 7 8 1 4 2 5 5 1 4 7 7 8 *